PRAISE FOR
How Do You Want to Show Up?

"This must-read book teaches critical leadership skills through people stories that keep the pages turning. Readers can use this book to strengthen their self-knowledge and improve communication at work and in the rest of life."

—Marshall Goldsmith, international bestselling author and editor of thirty-five books, including *What Got You Here Won't Get You There* and *Triggers*

"As she teaches self-reflection, Melissa helps her clients become more intentional as leaders. This book—and her engaging stories of coaching—shows readers how to do the same."

—Tom Ennis, CEO at Amplify Snack Brands and SkinnyPop Popcorn

"This is a compelling book that furthers our understanding of our own internal barriers and how each of us can overcome them. Melissa's vibrant storytelling ability keeps you turning the pages and deepens your self-awareness. She's one of the best in the coaching business and will help you succeed."

—Mark A. Finkelstein, former general counsel and executive vice president of corporate development at Emeritus Corporation

"There's something for everyone in *How Do You Want to Show Up?* Whether you're a seasoned executive or a young professional looking to find your voice and place in an organization, this book provides thoughtful insights and lessons that can help anyone advance their career."

—Michelle Rhee, former chancellor of the
Washington, DC, public schools

"Incredibly compelling storytelling that marvelously brings each coaching case to life. Which example are you?"

—Brian O. Underhill, PhD, founder and CEO of CoachSource
and author of *Executive Coaching for Results: The Definitive
Guide to Developing Organizational Leaders*

"Having had the opportunity to work directly with Melissa and experience positive results both personally and professionally, I know this book is a must-have for any professional looking to accelerate their career and impact their personal brand in a positive way."

—Chief executive officer at a global wellness consulting company

"Melissa's perceptive and masterful coaching help clients unlock their inner truths, which opens the door to self-knowledge, confidence, and ultimately power."

—Former vice president of marketing at a leading coffee retailer

"Whatever your leadership struggle—team dynamics, difficult conversations, advocating for yourself—this book shows how to overcome the problem by identifying and navigating your inner truths. Melissa has worked with our teams over the years and has led them through the conversations that are talked about in the book."

—Ron Inman, executive vice president at
Northwest Cascade and Honey Bucket

"Every reader will find inspiration and tools in Melissa's book. Her coaching has been instrumental in my career, and now she can share her expertise with the masses!"

—Distinguished program manager executive at a leading tech company in Seattle

"After two decades of leading teams and organizations (and despite some skepticism on my part), Melissa helped me break through and become a more effective leader. It was a very difficult but enlightening journey."

—Executive at a Fortune 50 company

"Melissa's warm, wise coaching helps clients understand their barriers to leadership. The stories and tools in her book can do the same for readers."

—Marty Diklich, president and CEO at AA Asphalting and former regional vice president at Masco Corporation and Milgard Windows and Doors

"A captivating book about understanding our internal barriers and how to unstick them. Melissa's coaching helped me understand my own leadership challenges and how to overcome them. Her book, *How Do You Want to Show Up?*, is a great new resource for executives and their employees."

—Sherri Mason, IT program manager at a leading management consulting company

"Melissa is an incredibly insightful coach, able to hone in on opportunities for development needed to take your leadership to the next level."

—Vice president of global customer experience at a multinational software corporation

"Melissa's superb storytelling and incredible insight takes the reader on a powerful journey toward greater self-knowledge and what it means to be human. The wisdom infused throughout this book is relevant and hugely beneficial to any reader!"

—Suzi Skinner, MCC, author of *Build Your Leader Identity*

"A thoughtful and approachable book, *How Do You Want to Show Up?* addresses many of the foundational skill sets leaders require to be effective. The lessons around self-awareness, authenticity, accountability, presence, difficult conversations, and more are spot-on characteristics of the best leaders we know."

—Michael Humphries, president at Waldron

"Melissa's examples of executives' challenges are relevant, while her solutions are practical and realistic."

—Former executive and current board member
at an independent review board

HOW DO YOU WANT
TO SHOW UP?

HOW DO YOU WANT TO SHOW UP?

Find Your Inner Truths—and Lead with Them

MELISSA WILLIAMS-GURIAN

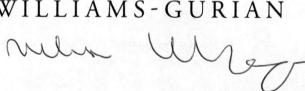

Published by Melissa Williams-Gurian, Seattle
www.melissawilliamsgurian.com

 Edited and Designed by Girl Friday Productions
www.girlfridayproductions.com

Editorial: Nicole Burns-Ascue
Interior Design: Paul Barrett
Cover Design: Anna Curtis
Author photo © 2013 Ingrid Pape-Sheldon Photography

ISBN (Hardcover): 978-0-9989051-1-2
ISBN (Paperback): 978-0-9989051-0-5
e-ISBN: 978-0-9989051-2-9

Library of Congress Control Number: 2017911499

CONTENTS

AUTHOR'S NOTE

IN MY COACHING WORK, I follow professional guidelines I
have learned over years of training and experience. It is important to know that coaching is an art that must at times adapt to
the particular needs of the individual and the context of the
situation or organization.

Characters, situations, and dialogue in this book are fictional and may not correspond perfectly to what would happen in any particular coaching session.

Where requested, contributors of testimonials and praise
have been made anonymous.

ACKNOWLEDGMENTS

I AM GRATEFUL FOR MY FAMILY: Randy, Tally, Coby, and Brandy, who inspire me to be my best and whose conversations I cherish in the car, on our hikes, and at the dinner table.

My dad, for providing the best training ground for me to observe, to truly listen, and to learn how to be with employees.

My brother, David, who says, "Just do it."

Maria, my thought leader, who helped me get ideas on paper.

My clients, from whom I learn much and who help me to be all that I am. I am grateful for our journey together; I see in you what I see in me.

And to you, the reader. I hope this book inspires you to have conversations with yourself and others to show up in the world as intended and to be all you were meant to be.

SECRETS OF A LEADERSHIP COACH

When you do things from your soul, you feel a river moving in you, joy.

—Rumi

I am not yet able . . . to know myself; so it seems to me ridiculous, when I do not yet know that, to investigate irrelevant things.

—Socrates

I WAS BORN INTO A family business. My father owned a chain of Hallmark stores in Maryland, in the suburbs of Washington, DC. Beginning at a young age, I would sometimes tag along to his stores, where I'd witness his leadership skills firsthand. I observed the respect with which he treated his employees and the creative ways he handled daily challenges. At the dinner table, he and my mother would talk about his work, and he would solicit her thoughts about larger decisions.

Later, starting around age twelve, I helped out in his stores after school. This, my first unofficial job, was my chance to learn about the working world. What I experienced there eventually led me to the work I am so passionate about now: coaching CEOs, senior management, and their teams.

Looking back, what was surprising about working in his stores was that my favorite ones were the busiest and seemed to have the best managers. I found myself studying what made these managers so good at their jobs. It didn't seem to be about the particular personality of each manager, because each was very different from another. One manager I liked a lot—I'll call her Susan—was outgoing, even loud, and at first she made me nervous. But I quickly warmed to her forthright manner, whether it was with a customer who had a complaint or a cashier who made frequent errors and arrived late to work. Another good manager, Terence, was quiet and kept the music in the store low, but he dressed crisply, stood proudly, knew something about every single store product, and noticed and acknowledged employees' work with praise or a kind smile.

Later, in adolescence, I worked at other retail stores and offices and saw other, more disastrous kinds of management.

All of it fascinated me—and still does. I love to think about the human factor in business and solve the question of how that can be harnessed to create wonderful organizations where employees work in thriving teams and produce high-caliber work.

This book is a result of real experiences I've had coaching top executives and helping to build high-performing teams for Fortune 500 companies, academic institutions, nonprofits, health care organizations, and other businesses. Leaders can grow lonely as they climb higher in an organization, and I want to share and normalize the many traits that leaders have in common. I also want to help leaders develop one of the traits I believe is central to long-term success in the workplace.

I observed it in my dad's stores, and I see it even more clearly now after twenty years of coaching leaders: one of the most important traits of truly effective leaders is self-knowledge. If you know yourself, your values, and how you want to show up in the world, you will inspire others, whether you are a noisy extrovert or radiate a quieter authority.

Successful leaders who are willing to do the work of knowing themselves are able to support others and navigate work relationships and organizational systems effectively. Leaders with self-knowledge are able to have conversations that matter.

There are so many important conversations that never take place in organizations, whether they are between a boss and a direct report or between two peers, and it is for the lack of these conversations that many businesses falter. Looking back at my dad's store managers, what did Susan and Terence, two such different people, have in common? They were both effective communicators, because they knew themselves well. Susan's style was somewhat brash, but she was wonderfully effective at communicating with clarity, directness, and compassion when problems arose. Soft-spoken Terence was terrific at reaching out to other employees almost daily to maintain connections and skillfully acknowledge good work. Susan's strength was that she could have the kinds of conversations most people avoid, at work or at home, because they can feel uncomfortable. Terence's strength was based in his quiet confidence and a generosity of spirit that allowed him to see and praise the efforts of employees. In both cases, they were having conversations that mattered.

I doubt that either of these managers had had any coaching. We all know people who seem to have been born with particularly good social and emotional skills. Sometimes they really are born that way, and sometimes they are raised in a way that has developed those skills. Yet even those natural experts at times face the challenge of how to communicate effectively. Human relationships are inherently difficult, and we make these relationships even harder given our internal barriers to communicating with others, such as fear, conflict avoidance, perfectionist tendencies, and a desire to be liked.

The good news is that, even for those of us who weren't born with self-insight or a brilliant communication style, these skills are teachable. I know, because daily I help some of the smartest leaders in the world get to know themselves and communicate more effectively in the workplace.

———

How Do You Want to Show Up? is the result of my more than twenty years of coaching executives and working as a therapist in private practice.

1. What is it you really believe?
2. What is it you really want?
3. What is it you are here to do?

Many of us start our careers with satisfying answers to these questions but stray off course. Or we never ask the questions in the first place. As we rise in our careers, we become so busy we forget to assess our performance to ensure we are bringing our true, full selves to the work we do.

No matter how talented we are, when we don't take the time to know ourselves and have those conversations, we don't work to our full capacity.

Companies hire me for many reasons, but the primary one is that they'd like to invest further in one of their employees who is doing exceptional work. I am brought in to help rising stars further develop their talents, perhaps to prepare them for a position with more responsibility.

Alternatively, I'm hired because an employee or team is in crisis. Perhaps someone has received a bad review or is on the brink of losing their job. The company hires me to coach the employee to change.

Sometimes I may work with my clients for a year or more, but often I am asked to accomplish substantial change in a shorter time frame, and I have seen clients make enormous changes in even a few short weeks. How?

Leaders are often surprised when I ask them to name their feelings, a subject not often crossed in offices and meeting rooms. (And when I say they're surprised, I mean that I regularly hear versions of "You've got to be kidding me" and "No, thanks.") But feelings get to the heart of the matter, and it is when we acknowledge them that we are most alive. Without a connection to our inner truths, our connection to others will falter. At best, we move forward in our work but find ourselves less inspired and more frustrated. At worst, our lack of self-knowledge contributes to the kind of work culture that can drag a business down.

On the other hand, when leaders know themselves and use that knowledge to communicate more effectively, it brings measurable business results.

A few common results I see in my work include:

1. Productivity soars in teams that are able to stop working in silo and have open, frank conversations.
2. Employees who sense an openness to sharing their full selves feel empowered to share ideas, leading to innovations.
3. People produce more and work harder when they are invested in their work, a feeling that comes about when they feel truly seen and acknowledged.

Many businesses know this, and the successful companies I work with are eager for tools to teach self-awareness and emotional intelligence to their top employees.

In *How Do You Want to Show Up?* I share stories from my coaching experiences with high-level executives. I hope to normalize many of the common challenges in the workplace that readers may be experiencing. They may find themselves in meetings dominated by the loudest person or bogged down by passive-aggressive behavior. Perhaps they are introverts who feel stuck, or extroverts who look like they have it all together but are, in fact, overextended. Many leaders are looking for new ways to resolve the conflicts that arise in every business. What my stories have in common is that these leaders, with coaching, were able to achieve their goals by becoming more self-aware and using that knowledge to have conversations that matter.

Sidebars throughout the book offer readers the tools and strategies I regularly use to help clients unlock self-awareness and move forward in their conversations—and their careers—with worksheets, graphics, and stories from the field.

This book includes materials I've developed or adapted over the past twenty years to guide my clients and organizations through the coaching process. Sidebars and graphic tools help readers work through their challenges, improve self-knowledge, and communicate more clearly.

Readers may find specific chapters addressing their own leadership challenges but can find materials in any chapter that are applicable to most leaders.

How to Use This Book

Read the stories about some of the leaders I've met and how we worked together to help them boost their self-knowledge, emotional intelligence, and communication skills, and you will find support for the common challenges leaders face. These are fictional characters and situations drawn from my real-life experiences of high-level coaching and include the following:

1. The brilliant executive whose chilly demeanor and critical responses were demoralizing her team until we helped her find her warmer side
2. The team of triangles, where no employee was able to give another direct feedback until the leader learned the secret to breaking a triangle
3. The high-achieving introvert who hadn't quite moved up on the job and worked to learn strategies for connecting with others on terms where he felt comfortable

Throughout, look for the tools I use to help leaders in the workplace achieve high performance for themselves and their teams.

TACKLING THE ELEPHANT IN THE ROOM

"I just want to get this over with."

MY CLIENT, ALEX, CHIEF DATA scientist at a major tech company, dropped into a chair in the conference room. He moved stiffly after a long run, his stress reliever of choice before awful meetings. Like nearly every meeting with his boss, John. Outside the window in front of him, a bank of Northern California fog rolled in. Behind him was the ubiquitous whiteboard.

"I understand," I said. I knew why Alex felt nervous, and I didn't blame him. Today, in a meeting with his boss—with me standing by to help steer the conversation if necessary—Alex would outline what he and I had accomplished in our coaching sessions so far. I didn't want to make any promises to him about the meeting's outcome, but I knew he was well-prepared, and I thought he would prevail.

Alex had been very open in our six months of meeting every two weeks. He'd told me exactly who he was—his family of origin, his background, his religion. I had coached him on setting career goals and helped him identify challenges. I'd also had opportunities to observe him with his team and had interviewed a dozen of his coworkers about his strengths and opportunities for growth. In our last sessions we had first talked about what I learned from those interviews, then met again to help him prepare to confront his boss.

Today was a chance for Alex to share the results of our work with the CEO. It was John, after all, who had asked me to talk to Alex, one of his most important and promising employees. "We need him, but his deliverables have to get better," John had told me in an email. "He does what we need, and he's really, really good at it, but he sometimes blows his deadlines," he said. "And he can't explain why. It's frustrating. I thought I was hiring a hard-charging bulldog of a guy. That's his reputation. But he doesn't seem to initiate much. He's just . . . quiet around me." To John, being too quiet was troubling. Speaking in dog terms again, John was more of a German shepherd, his bark almost deafening when he wanted to make a point. "I try to push him and challenge him to get him to speak up, but I'm not sure it's working," he concluded.

Reading that last point I'd felt a prickle on my neck, which made me think we might be approaching the root of the problem. Soon I'd learn just what that problem was. John's method was definitely not working. At all. And the blame did not lie entirely with Alex.

It was Alex's job to make this clear. Alex knew John would most likely challenge him on every assertion he made today as he told his boss what his own strengths were at the company and about his new goals and the progress he'd made in our coaching time. That, in itself, was stressful to anticipate. But the hardest part would come after that discussion. Alex had something urgent to tell John, and we both suspected it wouldn't go over well, at least at first.

Alex had to tell his boss that he had been acting like a jerk. Furthermore, that if John didn't improve his behavior, Alex would leave the company. John's arrogant attitude wasn't acceptable to Alex anymore.

I was sorry Alex was feeling stress and, I had to admit, I wanted to get this over with too. For reasons I'll describe shortly, John was not an easy man to confront, and I suspected this meeting probably wouldn't be an easy one.

Although it had taken weeks of coaching for Alex to begin to recognize it, I believed he had everything to gain from this uncomfortable conversation. The critical importance of such conversations is so much a part of my work with high-level executives that I sometimes forget this incredible truth: it isn't usually more money, more employees, or more of anything else the company doesn't already have that will make the biggest difference to a team. Often, what can help a team most is the conversation, or conversations, that bring what is already present out into the open.

If everyone could show up and state their truths, needs, and desires at any given moment, learn to sit with others' discomfort, and then move to action, we would all create our best selves.

Alex had astonishing raw talent. He studied analytics at one of the top two schools in the country and had already spent several years in charge of the data analysis at a Fortune 500 company.

My interviews with employees had also revealed he had incredible emotional intelligence when it came to dealing with others. I had rarely seen a team admire their boss more than his team admired Alex. "Caring," "approachable," "humble," and "egoless" met with "tactical," "brilliant," and "highly effective" to create a profile that would attract the most powerful businesses. This company had scored big when they hired him. They paid him accordingly, though of course he had little time to enjoy his extravagant income.

Yet, as one team member after another admitted to me, there was just this one thing they wished they could improve about Alex: he was too passive with his boss. John's aggressive, haranguing personality demoralized everyone, and Alex seemed to let it happen, never standing up for the team and regularly allowing John to give them more work than they could realistically handle. They also noticed that after meetings with John, Alex became short-tempered, and his stress had a ripple effect on everyone else.

John had a tendency to ask questions in a way that felt like an interrogation. He also did something I'd rarely seen at another business before.

"When I give a presentation to the company, half the time John doesn't even back me up," Alex told me. "Not only that, but he actually will start picking on me—or, well, it feels like picking on me—at the meeting."

I asked for examples.

"Like he'll say, 'Are you sure that chart is accurate?' or 'Where did you get those figures?'"

Alex closed his eyes briefly, as if his boss were saying those things at that very moment.

"What do you do then?" I asked.

"What can I do?" he said. "He's never going to listen to me. So I suck it up and look forward to another punishing run after work to relieve the tension." Alex felt sure that some things needed changing—for instance, more hires—but he didn't want to speak up only to be shot down. So he stayed quiet in meetings and let his boss dominate, while inwardly seething.

Today he would finally talk to John, and I'd coached him to work on speaking with clarity rather than letting the volcano blow all at once. Alex had told me that the team sat in assigned seats at meetings, so I now recommended to Alex that he sit in a different chair than his usual. I suggested we take seats at the middle of the long table, because then his boss would not have the option of claiming the head of the table, as could happen if Alex sat near one end. It was a symbolic move, but in my business, that can be important too. The two would appear on equal footing.

I knew the stale office air would soon feel charged.

When his boss came into the room, shook my hand firmly, and waited for me to take a seat before grabbing his own, Alex and I both experienced what everyone experiences around John.

I have worked with many high-level executives, and Alex's boss is one of only a very few leaders who have what I call the "it" factor. Not only is he charismatic and razor sharp, but he has a kind of magnetic energy that leads people to crave his approval. It's not the normal feeling of wanting to please the boss, but something so powerful that when you work with him, you have a hard time remembering your own opinion. If John says it's true, it must be true.

I've spent some time thinking about this rare "it" factor and, in John's case, I sensed that it came from a certain kind of withholding. He didn't seem cold, but he did seem invulnerable, and he was very hard to please. He rarely said thank you or showed appreciation.

In our culture we like to think of that aggressive, invulnerable personality as an asset in business. Certainly charisma and magnetism can draw a crowd. Yet John stood to potentially lose at least one outstanding employee because he didn't recognize how he came across, nor did he realize the importance of listening to his team and encouraging feedback. In this situation, his magnetism actually worked against the company's long-term success. As he acted invulnerable, it left little opening for others to feel safe to express weakness or uncertainty. As he dominated every conversation, quieter team members weren't given the space to come forward, which meant that he was missing out on valuable information and not getting all he could from the people he had helped to hire.

We can all finesse the personalities we already have, but what we need first is to see ourselves more clearly. John really didn't know, but Alex was about to tell him.

John sat across from Alex, and I sat beside John. I had already coached John several times in other situations, so we were used to a comfortable collegiality, but today I was there to help Alex hold steady and state his differences in the face of the magnetic "it."

True to the character his team had described, Alex first acknowledged me and offered praise for my coaching. Then he opened the conversation with his boss.

"You've been through this kind of meeting a few times now," Alex said. "What do you think is the best way to have this conversation today?"

Silence.

It would have been easy for me to say something in that moment to break the ice, but I stayed quiet.

Finally John spoke. "Let's just walk through it," he said.

I suspected he didn't realize that Alex was going to take his first-ever opportunity to cut through the "it" factor and give John some observations of his own. As Alex described his accomplishments, John aggressively queried him.

"I have a high-performing team," said Alex.

"You think so?" countered John. "You think you have a high-performing team?"

"Yes, I do," said Alex.

"Tell me, who on the team do you think is high-performing?" said John.

The presentation of Alex's coaching work and future goals went on like this for twenty minutes until it was time for us to move on to the trouble between Alex and John.

"One of the things that came up in the feedback from the interviews was our relationship," said Alex. Alex brought up the dynamic between them: the interrupting at meetings and the lack of appreciation he showed for Alex's work. As John looked at him with raised eyebrows, Alex summed it all up.

"Sometimes, John, you can be an asshole."

I heard John's breath get shallow. He squeezed his hands into fists. "No one here has ever told me that," he said to Alex. His voice stayed even. "No one else has said this, and I don't believe it."

"I know it's not just me. You're a jerk to others too," said Alex.

Based on the feedback I had received from colleagues about John when he went through his own coaching, this was true.

After a moment of silence, seeing that Alex had not even come close to deflating and wasn't planning to soften his statements, I decided it was a fine time for me to step in.

"Of all the subjects I've covered with the team, the most overwhelming feedback I've gotten has been about this dynamic between you two," I said.

Bomb number two.

John's eyes narrowed. "I can't believe that," he said.

Silence.

"Well, I can see maybe a couple instances where possibly my feedback was too strong. But it wasn't personal," he said, relenting.

Alex said, "Whatever you think, I need this to change. It's very important for me. In fact, it's a deal breaker. I can't stay in this job if you continue to treat me this way."

John went on the defensive again. "This feedback didn't show up in the meetings I had with other employees." He had had several meetings already like the one we were having today, but I knew he wasn't done with all of them, and I pointed that out.

"Well, that's true," he said.

That was a crack in his defense, and he seemed to be ready to hear more. Alex gave him a few examples of behavior that had alienated him, and after a few minutes of discussion, John began to nod occasionally or take a note.

The conversation became more open, and John breathed more easily.

"I can now see some of those moments," John finally said. We had taken the first step toward change.

This was a terrific beginning and a home run for my client. I wasn't sure that John knew everything he'd signed up for, but he wasn't the only one who had work to do. Alex had gotten to this meeting after a lot of hard work in our coaching meetings, and he had more to do to make sure he held his boundaries in the future.

MANAGING CONVERSATIONS, PARTICULARLY DIFFICULT ONES

We all need extra help with difficult conversations. In a 2013 Stanford Business School executive-coaching survey, the highest area of concern regarding personal development for CEOs was learning skills for conflict management, and I personally haven't met a leader who was entirely comfortable with one-on-one, high-conflict conversations. Yet avoiding high-conflict conversations can be disastrous for a business.

In every conversation we manage three parts: ourselves, the message, and the person or group we are addressing. Effective communication starts with the understanding that there is my point of view (my truth), and someone else's point of view (their truth).

CONVERSATION

In every conversation, we manage three parts

OURSELVES	THE MESSAGE	THEM
Think	Intent	(in regard to what we said)
Feel	Body language	Think
Want	Tone	Feel
		Want

Effective communication starts with the understanding that there is my
point of view *(my truth) and* someone else's point of view *(their truth).*
Rarely is there absolute truth.

There are communication skills that make conversations easier and more effective while keeping both truths in mind.

———

Alex's work in coaching had been intense at times, but I wasn't surprised that he'd broken through to challenge his boss, which was a conversation that was a couple of years overdue. During our work together I'd seen not only Alex's brilliance but also a determination that led him to work through barriers and move forward. One of the early challenges was when I brought out a deceptively easy tool that can prove to be a huge hurdle—akin to the looming walls and lumpy mud pits in one of those popular obstacle races. It's called the "feeling chart," and it is a chart I bring to some meetings that lists about twenty-five different possible feelings. Though it sounds simple, when the chart is put into use, it can be a very powerful document.

FEELINGS CHART

INTENSITY OF FEELINGS	GLAD	SAD	MAD	AFRAID	ASHAMED
HIGH	Elated Excited Overjoyed Thrilled Exuberant Ecstatic Fired Up Delighted	Depressed Disappointed Alone Hurt Dejected Hopeless Sorrowful Miserable	Furious Enraged Outraged Aggravated Irate Seething	Terrified Horrified Scared Stiff Petrified Fearful Panicky	Sorrowful Remorseful Unworthy Worthless Disgraced Dishonored
MEDIUM	Cheerful Up Good Relieved Satisfied	Heartbroken Down Upset Distressed Regretful Melancholy	Upset Mad Hot Frustrated Agitated Disgusted	Scared Frightened Threatened Insecure Uneasy Shocked	Apologetic Defamed Sneaky Guilty
MILD	Content Pleasant Pleased	Unhappy Blue Lost Bad Dissatisfied	Perturbed Annoyed Uptight Put Out Irritated Touchy	Apprehensive Nervous Worried Timid Unsure Anxious	Embarrassed Disappointed Let Down

Still, most people can't see the value of this chart right away. When I ask a client to look at it and identify which feeling they are having now or which they may have had at some important moment in their workday, they look at me like they are suddenly reassessing my professional ability. "Seriously?" they say. "Is this really necessary?"

In Alex's case, I brought out the feeling chart so I could learn how he felt in the moments when John publicly questioned his ability. I also wanted to know what he usually felt when he knew he was missing a deadline John had given him.

I started with the moments when John was undermining him.

"What do you feel at those times?" I asked.

Alex looked at the chart.

"Pretty much everything under the 'Mad' column," he said. "Furious, seething, mad, agitated, put out—you name it."

"Okay," I said, jotting down his answer in my notes. Usually we sit with the chart for a while, because often I find my clients refine their assessments after they've thought a little more deeply.

We moved on to how he felt when he was missing a deadline. He had already told me the reasons he couldn't keep on top of his work: his boss was throwing too much at him, and he couldn't push it all onto his team. Since John was already breathing down his neck, he didn't feel he could argue for less work, though he did think the workload was unreasonable.

"Why aren't you getting it done?" I'd ask.

And he'd say, "I guess that's my rebellion."

So how did he feel?

"Well, I'm not sure I have a feeling about it," he said. "I just can't keep up."

I suggested he try to recall a recent moment when he opened an email and saw that his boss wanted to add more to his already impossibly full plate.

John wanted Alex to do what he asked, because getting results from his team made him feel effective. But Alex, whose own intelligence and work were not getting proper recognition, fought back by not doing what was asked of him. It was a classic passive-aggressive situation.

Alex's rebellion was passive. For example, the two of them had agreed that Alex would send his boss weekly updates. Alex would then learn that his boss wasn't reading them. This understandably pissed off Alex, so he stopped sending emails. When John finally noticed this, he was unhappy that Alex had stopped updating him.

"You agreed to do this," John told him. "I need these now."

"You're not reading them, so why does it matter?" asked Alex.

While I understood Alex's frustration, John's argument made sense. They had made an agreement, and Alex had the responsibility. John had never promised to read the emails. I suspected Alex knew he was still responsible for this task no matter what response he got or didn't get. He needed to hold himself accountable for what he'd agreed to or else change the terms.

"Would you want to renegotiate with John to agree that you'll only keep sending the emails as long as he will read them within the week?" I asked.

Alex seemed to back down. "No, I don't want to go that far," he said. "I just want to know that my time is being valued."

"So when he doesn't read the emails, you feel your time is being taken for granted?"

"Yes," he said.

I showed him the chart again. Did he see any feelings there that came up when he imagined his boss was not valuing his time? What did he feel when he thought about writing an update, then changed his mind? Was he just forgetful?

"No, I'm not really forgetful," he said.

I knew that. Alex was very sharp and organized.

He looked at the paper again. "I guess I'd say defiant," he said. "I'm kind of embarrassed to admit it, though."

"Why?" I asked.

"Because in other parts of my life I would be more direct. But for some reason, with my boss, I guess I just want to be as rude to him as he is to me even though I know it won't get us anywhere."

Alex and I talked about that defiant feeling. It suggested to me that he knew in advance he wasn't going to do the work his boss set out for him, yet he still wasn't willing to tell his boss that his workload was unreasonable. Instead he was choosing to ignore John's assignments. He didn't realize this was a form of giving up, but it was.

The feeling chart, then, is useful to help a person notice not just their actions but also the underlying motivation for their actions. Alex isn't only overburdened, but he's angry and embarrassed too. He is showing his anger in a way that takes away his power. Passive-aggressive relationships can leave employees feeling negative and unmotivated. And these employees often bring the problems home, so the tension permeates life and drags down energy. In this case, it also affected everyone on Alex's team and affected the business. Everyone felt a bit awkward, and no one could quite be themselves.

Every step you can take toward addressing what is true for you directly, rather than indirectly, helps you gain in power and self-confidence.

And the closer you can get to doing that *in the moment* rather than a week or a month later, the more effective it will be.

Alex needed to be direct with John, but first he'd have to figure out why he was unable to hold a boundary with his boss, whether it was letting John know that he needed to be treated better or letting him know that his demands were unreasonable.

"How do you feel when someone on your team tells you they think John is piling too much work onto everyone?" I asked.

Alex looked at the chart again. "Embarrassed," he said. "And apologetic."

I knew it was important for him to take direct action with John, not stay stuck in reacting. "Are you willing to talk openly with him about your needs?" I asked. "Is that something you are willing to do?"

"Maybe," said Alex, "but I don't think he'll listen. I've tried before, and it didn't get me anywhere."

I listened to Alex push back on the idea of having this difficult conversation, and I thought about what clients in the past had said about hard conversations that had ultimately led to a positive shift in their situations. I'd hit upon a few questions that could help a person make the decision about whether or not to have that difficult conversation. Some of the questions I think worth asking are:

1. If I don't have the conversation, how will I feel?
2. Is there something in particular I want from this conversation? Do I think I will I get it?
3. Even if I don't get that concrete result, is it important to my values to have the conversation? For instance, do I value authenticity and feel that a discussion will bring me closer to an authentic connection with another person? Do I believe in being supportive and know that having this conversation could be helpful to another?

———

I didn't mention these questions directly to Alex now, because I felt there was another direction we could take that might help him clarify what to do.

My clients seem to expect me to ask about their families of origin, perhaps because they know I have a background as a counselor. In fact, some people choose me because they think my counseling background is an added benefit to working with me. I think we can find clues to why we act as we do at work when we consider our position and history with our first "team," our family. That information is part of how we discover our inner truths. Find those truths and we can ground ourselves: Ah, yes, *this* is who I am. *This* is what is important to me.

Understandably, bringing up families and childhood in executive coaching can also sometimes catch people off guard. Early on in our coaching sessions I had felt Alex might be the sort of person who would be resistant to opening up on this subject. But now, after he'd agreed to use the feeling chart and had expressed vulnerability in our conversations more than once, it seemed safe to dig into his family background. If we could uncover why he might feel unable to confront his boss, we would likely be able to leapfrog to helping Alex feel more comfortable actually doing so.

We needed to move on from the very real problems of John's leadership style to find out why Alex was accepting a boss who walked all over him.

Had he had a tough time setting boundaries like this since he was younger or was it specific to this job?

"How did your family communicate when you were growing up?" I asked him.

"Not so well," he said.

"Did you debate in your family or argue at all?"

He didn't hesitate to answer. "I didn't debate or argue," he said. "I didn't want my dad to know more about me than he had to. And my mom would never challenge my dad. She didn't dare." Alex leaned back in his chair and began opening up about his childhood. He told me about a father who was too involved in his life—he pressured him to work harder, even when Alex was getting some of the top grades in his class. He regularly rifled through Alex's things looking for evidence that he wasn't the perfect child he seemed to be. His mother was withdrawn. Alex's pivotal moment was when he decided to move away to a college across the country despite his father's insistence that he must stay nearby. Alex had managed to win a full scholarship and, against difficult odds—including some undermining moves by his father—he'd worked hard to cover his extra costs with work-study jobs.

MELISSA WILLIAMS-GURIAN

"So you didn't argue with him," I said. But it was also clear that he had not acquiesced to his father's demands. "Was there ever a time you stood up to him?"

He thought for a minute and then said, "Yes. It was in a letter."

Alex's father had never let up with criticisms of his choice to move away to college, and it wasn't until a couple of years after he graduated that Alex was at last able to tell him, in a letter, that his dad wasn't allowed to do that anymore if he wanted to hear from his son again.

"How were you able to do that?" I asked.

"Well, I never felt that great around my father, so I guess I knew there was more at stake for him than for me. It wasn't easy, but I felt confident that I would be okay either way."

"Did anyone support you in that move?" I asked.

"My girlfriend at the time was supportive," he said. "And," he continued, "I also remembered something I'd learned from a counselor at college."

I nodded encouragingly. He was clearly sharing something important.

"I was told I had anxiety," he said. He told the story. Alex had been carrying a heavy load at his demanding university and one night, after not enough sleep, he found himself lying on the floor unable to breathe very well, feeling a bit like he was detached from his body and the rest of reality. He was panicked, but at the same time the feeling was familiar. He'd had several such attacks growing up but never had anyone to help him. This time his roommate—a caring person who was studying to become a doctor—urged him to see a counselor, who eventually helped Alex recognize that he had a tendency toward anxiety.

"The counselor told me then that one part of keeping anxiety at bay is to work on lowering the number of things that cause me stress. Since I couldn't cut back on school—that's just not in my nature—we talked about social events I said yes to

24

when I wanted to say no and committing to better sleep habits rather than letting myself pull all-nighters. We also talked about not letting other students lean on me. I had some group projects where other people were letting me do more of the work. Anyway, it finally hit me that my dad fell into the category of things that stress me out but offer me little. I knew if I didn't want to have more anxiety, I had to do it."

HOW OUR FAMILY OF ORIGIN AFFECTS WHO WE ARE NOW

The families we grew up with are with us long after we've gone out on our own. Understanding past influences is not always necessary to making changes in the present but can help reveal unconscious patterns and assist a leader in the kind of self-knowledge that creates lasting change. In coaching leaders, certain background and family-of-origin dynamics seem to regularly bubble to the top. Want to know yourself better and how you show up in the world? Consider the following questions:

- How did your family manage conflict? How might that relate to how you manage it now?
- Are you an introvert or an extrovert? How did that fit into your family?
- Were you more of a close or a distant family, and how might that sort of connection show up at work?
- Was communication in your family more direct or indirect?
- What were the educations and careers of your parents? How might that have influenced who you are and who you want to be?
- Were there addictions in your family?
- Were there any major illnesses in siblings or parents?
- What kinds of boundaries were there in your family? Was it strict or lenient? Did your parents more often say yes or no?

> • What was your sibling position? Eldest, middle, or young-
>   est? Only?

Alex rose rapidly in federal government jobs after he graduated, and he says he was always able to please other bosses
he'd had in the past. This job, however, seemed to be testing
that ability.

"Have you ever been able to create a boundary with John?"
I asked.

He didn't think so, but then he remembered one time.

"Well, actually, when I first started working here, he did
try to make me stay later so we could meet about one thing or
another. It was pretty unpredictable. But I had already told him
when I signed that one thing that was important to me was
that I got home for my kids and wife most nights of the week.
When he started to ask for too many later evenings or work
dinners with clients, I told him that wasn't going to work."

"How did you do that?" I asked.

Alex, who had been serious up to this point, looked down
at the table between us and laughed.

"You know, it was hard at first. I told him I had personal
reasons for not being able to stay late, and he told me to suck it
up. In this case, I knew sucking it up was the wrong thing to do."

"So what did you do?" I asked again.

"I told him this was a nonnegotiable situation. Man, I had
to work to get those words out, but I'm glad I did. It worked."

"Great!" I said. I was relieved he'd already laid some groundwork by standing up to his boss in the past. "Can you think of
any other times you set boundaries like this?"

"Well," he said, "I've always been more interested in moving forward than getting involved in boundaries and negotia-
tions. Nothing comes to mind."

Finding examples of experiences in the past is a great way
to set groundwork for the future. Alex had previously been

successful at demanding and getting what he needed. Talking to John would be flexing a muscle he hadn't used in a while but not an entirely new experience.

"Are there other situations that would be clear enough that you would be willing to draw the line with him again?"

Alex said anything that interfered with his relationship with his family would be nonnegotiable, such as last-minute work trips that conflicted with important family events.

I wondered to myself whether the stress of working with his boss could be considered to be interfering with his family life. Alex seemed to be thinking the same thing.

"I guess it's possible that my problems with John could be getting to the point of interfering with my family life," he said.

"In what way?"

"Well, my wife has actually mentioned that I seem more short-tempered than usual," he said. "Sometimes I have to go exercise first instead of going straight home to see my kids, because I'm so frustrated I know I'm going to be hard to be around for a while."

Alex looked at the corner of the room, deep in thought. Then he turned back to me, raising his eyebrows.

"So if this is affecting my life with my family, does this mean it should be a nonnegotiable situation too?"

"Well, it's up to you," I said. "But does it feel like an option to let things with John continue in the same way, given that your job is having that effect?"

"No," he said. "I hadn't really thought about it before, but now that I do, this situation is nonnegotiable too."

But still he thought maybe it wasn't worth talking to his boss. Even though he couldn't go on like this, maybe eventually he'd just look for a new job. Why bother to confront him?

"You know, I doubt he'll change his behavior."

I knew differently. In a particular moment when it was really important to him, Alex had been able to set a boundary, and he had found that his boss respected that. But in day-to-day work he had not been able to do that consistently, and his boss kept asking for as much as he could get away with. Alex was highly valuable and not easily replaced. Of course, there was always a chance that John wouldn't change, but it was unlikely. Regardless of John's choice, asserting the boundary was bigger than this one situation. It was practicing self-leadership, a skill that is important in all aspects of our lives.

Leadership isn't just about leading others. It is also about leading yourself. Alex knew how to lead his team. But he was used to a formula that said that his boss, John, was leading, and he needed to follow. Even with a boss, we all need to tap into our inner compass. Similar to the awareness wheel featured in *Talking and Listening Together: Connecting with Self and Others* (1988) by Sherod Miller, Phyllis Miller, Elam W. Nunnally, and Daniel B. Wackman, our inner compass is those gut feelings that give us information we need to make decisions.

To make choices, we usually need to evaluate the facts, but the inner compass helps us sort out how we feel about those facts and how they align with our experiences and values.

Most of us, at one time or another, dismiss those gut feelings. We have all sorts of reasons for doing so. We're scared, or we don't really want to do the work required of us. (This happens a lot to storybook heroes at the beginning of a journey right before they accept a challenge and go on a wonderful adventure—think Bilbo Baggins.) Maybe we aren't willing to give up on a dream in which we've invested a lot of effort.

We all know this feeling of self-dismissal, and it looks something like what Alex had done earlier in our conversation:

Inner feeling: I've been tense all week. This feels awful.

Thought: I have got to talk to my boss about the workload. It's an unreasonable amount, and I can't keep up. I need to let him know and ask for changes.

Rationalization: Do I really need to talk to him? It's probably better just to suck it up and keep going. Maybe I'll quit later. He'll never change anyway.

Alex was tapping into his inner compass now, but he wasn't quite ready to follow it, and I was worried he would go even longer without changing. "To some extent you teach people how to treat you," I explained. "When you don't object to John's actions, you show that he can continue this way." It was unusually blunt for me, but the situation seemed to warrant it.

I knew it stung when I said it, because Alex raised his eyebrows in irritation, and I asked him what he thought about this idea. He wanted to blame his boss. And though his boss was behaving badly, Alex needed to understand the power of his own behavior before he could improve his situation.

"This is hard," he said. Then he nodded. "But this is good. It's probably what I needed to hear."

It's true that when you make a change, it's impossible to know how others will react. But that does not mean avoiding the conversation is better. In a way, it's still an unspoken conversation.

I decided to refocus on the reason we were here. "What do you want?" I asked Alex now. "How do you want to be treated by John?"

"I want to be respected," he replied. "Isn't that what we're talking about?" He looked at me like maybe I was a little denser than he'd realized.

I smiled. "I have done this work for a long time, and one thing I can tell you is that if you talk to your boss about what you need, there will be a shift in your relationship. It may not be exactly what you wanted, but you won't be stuck with the current norm."

He sighed. "I know I should talk to him," he said.

"If you want to," I told him. "It's really up to you."

All the work Alex had done paid off a couple of weeks later when he had the conversation that shifted the dynamic with John.

Where Is Alex Now?

Once Alex spoke up and held his ground, his self-awareness increased quickly. John, for his part, was a bit slow to accept that he had been mistreating Alex in a way that warranted being called a profanity, but John had a pretty sturdy ego. And Alex later said that he sensed his boss had, in some ways, appreciated being called out. Their relationship changed quickly. There were no more surprise attacks from John at meetings when Alex had the floor, and within a month Alex was able to negotiate plans for a new hire on his team so they were no longer overworked. Months later Alex got a new role and a new boss and, using skills he'd been practicing with John, immediately set a direct tone with the boss. Alex now shines in a role that is more demanding than ever before.

Reader Assignment

Ask yourself how you are showing up at work right now. Do you feel valued to the fullest? Or are you feeling similar to Alex—minimized and unsure what to do about it? Are there boundaries you need to more clearly define? What might those be? Do you need to have a conversation? If so, with whom? If you showed up more fully at work, what would that look like? What are the barriers—within yourself and also externally—for fully showing up at work right now?

SHARING YOUR AUTHENTIC SELF GRACEFULLY

IF ALEX WAS ALLOWING HIS authentic self to be suppressed by the boss, Ellen had no such problem.

I first met her in her office, a light-filled space in downtown Portland, Oregon, that reflected her financial success as a chief scientist and shareholder at a thriving medical company. The room was decorated with modern furnishings clearly selected by an interior designer: white Barcelona chair, clean-lined leather couch, a sleek credenza to hold her many files. The floor looked freshly vacuumed, the windows squeaky clean. It all would have been even more beautiful if there hadn't been files piled on shelves and chairs, a stack of what appeared to be unopened mail on her desk, and not one thing in the room—besides her impressive medical degrees—that looked as if it had been placed there by Ellen herself. No family photos, pet pictures, or knickknacks revealing a personality. The arrangement of cacti in interesting shapes—clearly installed by the designer in an effort to warm up the space—appeared to be withering from neglect.

Ellen showed up exactly as she was. She was stunningly brilliant and entirely practical, and had no time for niceties like maintaining order or even allowing an assistant to do so. No time for "warm touches" that weren't going to help her find a cure or save lives. Ellen had a strong preference for the cool honesty of facts.

What she didn't know was that practicing warmth and taking the time to have conversations were actually steps she would soon need to take in order to keep her business running.

Ellen had contacted me after the board of the company she worked for told her they wanted her to work with an executive coach. The board hadn't been clear about the reason, but they were clear on the seriousness of the problem. Employees had been complaining, and even the CEO and CFO avoided contact with her.

Ellen had interviewed several coaches before selecting me, and for our first few meetings I wondered if I was lucky or unlucky. I encountered Ellen's chilly, dismissive style more than once, and it gave me goose bumps. But as I have learned time and again in my work, with the right person and a lot of honesty that sometimes can only come through the window of unbiased coaching, even the chilliest person can become more adept at working with others.

For all the potential barriers to coaching Ellen, I soon learned something hopeful from her. She cared about the fact that people were unhappy with her.

"Well, I guess they don't like my work, but I don't understand why," she said at our first meeting, pushing a few email printouts at me. They were notes from the Human Resources department. I took the emails and told her I'd look them over later if she wanted, but first I wanted to talk to her a bit about what she thought might be the problem.

"I don't think my talking is very fruitful," she said. "I'm a scientist. The work I do is saving lives. You're the expert in your job. Give me the steps, and I'll take them."

She handed me the emails. I explained to her that the next step for me would be to gather anonymous feedback from the people she interacted with regularly at work to learn how they perceived her in their interactions. She nodded and said that would be fine. As she began to stand up to dismiss me, I said one more thing.

"This is your coaching, not mine, and I'd love to help you any way I can. What do you want for yourself in this process?"

She had been halfway out of the chair, but now she sat down again. "I know I can probably work on how I communicate with people," she said. "But I don't know. Is that important? I know I do a good job at my work."

We sat with that for a minute. Sometimes the most important part of my work is waiting for my clients to come to their own conclusions without me butting in.

While I waited for more, she stood up again and stuck out her hand. "You're the expert. I need to get back to work. Let me know what I can do, and I'll do it."

Well, at least she was agreeable.

Much of her work was in the lab, it's true. But she also needed to interact with people such as her support staff, the CFO, and Human Resources. I asked Ellen for a list of people she worked with regularly so that I could conduct my interviews—that process of collecting feedback from coworkers that I do for most clients. One big difference between private therapy and this kind of coaching is that the coach learns about the "coachee" not only from the client herself, but also from reports of others who have worked with her. This can be a painful process for the client, but I think it can also be a wonderful, life-transforming experience. We often wonder how we're perceived, and this is a rare opportunity to hear the unvarnished truth. Ellen really needed to hear the truth if she wanted to continue at this company, and it would also be important if she worked elsewhere.

I let Ellen choose the coworkers I should talk to so she could feel some agency over this uncomfortable process.

During those feedback interviews, I heard almost uniformly from those who worked with her that she was brusque and communicated poorly. The responses were even more critical than I expected. Sayid, one of her lab employees, had worked with her for six months and told me—after I assured him his words would be confidential—that he tried to avoid contact with Ellen if at all possible. As he sat across from me in the office one day while Ellen was out for one of her rare off-site visits, he pressed his hands to his temples a couple of times as if still feeling the headaches he told me he got during tense days with Ellen.

"Does she give you feedback?" I asked.

"If you can call 'That will work' feedback," he said.

"What does she say if you do a job particularly well?" I asked.

"I doubt she ever thinks I do a job particularly well," he said.

During another interview, a member of the board who had known Ellen for several years in a working capacity told me that when his wife died after a long illness and he sent an email around to the group to let them know, Ellen had replied a day after everyone else and her note was two sentences long: "Sorry for your loss. Let us know how many board meetings you'll miss."

I'd like to say I was floored, but this wasn't the first time I'd seen a person with intellectual brilliance stumble badly in the category of emotional intelligence. In my jobs as a coach and therapist, I'm well aware there are many different ways of being smart, and that many people—often the ones we think of as the smartest—have spectacular blind spots.

I generally get called into a situation either because an executive wants a high-performing team and feels the team is struggling or because someone is new in their role and the executive wants to set the groundwork that will help them become an exceptional leader. In some cases, I am called in because there are serious problems or signs of pain among employees in the organization. Sometimes the trouble is that a person is dragging down the company and isn't going to change. Perhaps they should have been fired a long time ago, and I am there for the final steps to confirm that firing is the right thing to do. Even more of the time I'm called because the company really wants to invest in a person. The company just loves the employee's work and wants to support them in every way.

Ellen fell somewhere in the middle. Her work, as she had accurately assessed, was important science and she performed it well, so it would be tough to oust her. But even scientists need to know how to have contact with other people, and Ellen did not. Would she be able to change with the feedback I was going to give her? That question nagged at me quite a bit.

Our intentions are invisible. People only see behavior. This accounts for many of the gaps we experience between how we see ourselves and how the world sees us.

I had a sense that perhaps Ellen's intentions were better than how they appeared from her behavior. Perhaps she really didn't care about her impact on others, yet I already knew she was surprised and upset by the negative feedback from HR, so I suspected that she probably did care. I was certain she cared about her company, and obviously she was good at learning.

I wasn't sure if I'd be able to teach her emotional intelligence. We'd start by faking it, which, as we've all heard, can be the first step to making it.

———

Some people project warmth without effort and understand intuitively how to connect with others. These traits often serve those lucky people well throughout their lives. While there can be other sides to connecting easily with others, such as shallowness—sociopaths can be charming, smooth talkers!—overall, being able to connect with warmth and sociability is a coveted strength.

On the other hand, those who present themselves in a cool, even prickly, fashion seem doomed to be less successful in human relations. We rarely learn these social skills in school, so they can seem immutable. As my work with Ellen would reveal, that is not the case. Even adults can learn to project warmth and make better connections with others. And they can do it in their own style.

When I approached Ellen with the feedback I had gathered from her coworkers, she was devastated. Her arms were folded as she read the assessment, and she winced in spots. I even saw her hands start to shake, and her voice was trembling a bit as she tried to tell me how she felt. "I had no idea I came across this way," she said. "I really care about people, and that person they describe is nothing like who I want to be." There was a yawning gap between her inner self and how she was showing up in the world. The fact that it upset her was my first clue that perhaps we would be able to work something out.

When I'm presented with a situation like this and with limited time to change a lifetime of misunderstandings, I tend to go big. Sometimes going big means looking at the organization as a whole to see the bigger picture. In this case, I decided I would dig in to try to find out what was going on inside Ellen's mind.

"What would your siblings say about you?"

"I thought I knew, but now I really don't know."

"Are you willing to find out?" I asked.

"Sure, if that will help."

"I think it might." I thought perhaps I'd learn more by starting with her family of origin, and I asked her if we could call one of her sisters to see what she had to say. Ellen suggested we call her younger sister, who worked from home and might be available midday. She said she'd text her first just to see if it was okay. A few phone rings later we had Anna on the line.

"Anna, you're on speakerphone, and my coach is sitting right here," said Ellen.

"Oh! Hi, Melissa!" Anna said. She sounded cheerful but quick—a much warmer version of the reserved woman sitting across from me. Ellen had told her about me, and Anna, clearly more of a people person, had already memorized my name.

After greetings, Ellen got down to business.

"So, Melissa asked me how you would describe me, and I wasn't sure. Are you willing to tell her in front of me?" Ellen asked.

I was poised on the edge of my seat, curious about what I'd hear next.

"Can I be honest?" said Anna. "I don't want my big sis to get mad."

Anna had clearly also experienced Ellen's more difficult side.

"Please do be honest," said Ellen. "This is important." Her tone was serious.

"Well, when we were in high school, Ellen could intimidate people," she said.

I wasn't surprised.

Anna continued, "She intimidated me. But I also admired her. She's the smartest person I know."

Ellen's head was down, and she was taking notes like someone attending a college lecture.

With compliment in place, Anna launched into an honest assessment. Her voice became more hesitant as she explained that her sister was a matter-of-fact person who did not like to waste time, did not like it when people said foolish things, and did not hold back in arguments to save people's feelings. She rarely shared emotions. Sometimes, she said, Ellen could come across as harsh and defensive, even though Anna believed that Ellen meant well.

I saw Ellen wince as she kept taking notes.

"In many ways, I like it, though," added Anna. "I always know she's telling me the truth. Oh, and one more thing. I have to admit that at the end of most arguments, I usually realize she's right."

Anna also said that Ellen reminded her a little of their mother.

"We grew up in a loving household," she said, "but our mom was also very, very practical. When you think of Mom, what do you think of as one of her favorite phrases?" she asked Ellen.

"That's easy," said Ellen, laughing for perhaps the first time since I'd met her. "Life isn't fair. Get over it!"

I hoped she would keep her current job and not have a reason to use that saying again.

———

When we met again in her office, HR had given Ellen a list of changes she needed to make. She pushed the list across the table to me, just like before. The letter was short and to the point:

We have had complaints about how employees are being treated.
We need you to change the following:
Improved treatment of employees
Improvement of spoken and written communication

This kind of information wasn't specific enough or timely enough to be of real use to Ellen, but we would work with it.

As I read it, I looked up and saw Ellen open a plain black notebook, smooth a hand across the page, and set her pen on the paper.

"I bought a coaching book, as you suggested," she said. "I'm ready to work on this."

It wasn't warmth, exactly, but it filled me with hope for our work together.

I asked her for any updates since our last appointment. She told me that she and her sister had talked again on the phone.

"I asked her why she hadn't told me before," said Ellen. "She said, 'I thought you knew you were like that!'

"I was seriously embarrassed. People think I'm mean because I'm not warm, but I honestly do care. I grew up with a really nice family. My sister does think I'm a kind person. It's just that I learned to be very practical. Eldest child, science-minded. What can I say? I'm task-oriented! Now, can you give me some tasks I can do to get this problem figured out?"

She wasn't smiling about this yet, but I hoped one day, when she'd mastered some tricks to warming up her style, she would be able to see some humor in her blind spots. That's the best we can do. We *all* have blind spots, and we all have challenges as we learn how best to communicate with others. That's what it means to be human.

LEADING WITH WARMTH

The way to influence and lead begins with warmth. Warmth facilitates trust, communication, and absorption of ideas. Warmth demonstrates that I hear you, I understand you, and I can be trusted.

People often choose to lead with competence and not warmth, but in my experience, everyone wants to feel warmth from others. Research bears out my experience. In the article "Connect, Then Lead," (*Harvard Business Review*, July-August

2013) authors Amy Cuddy, Matthew Kohut, and John Neffinger describe behavioral research that suggests people may comply with the demands of a leader who is not warm, but privately are less likely to feel motivated to perform well for such a person than for a leader who, for instance, validates feelings, asks about others, and uses more open gestures. "Most leaders today tend to emphasize their strength, competence, and credentials in the workplace, but that is exactly the wrong approach," write the authors. "Leaders who project strength before establishing trust run the risk of eliciting fear and, along with it, a host of dysfunctional behaviors."

Sometimes I like to think of this question of warmth or coolness as the act of learning your own emotional temperature. Where do you fall on the thermometer? (And did you know that you probably fall even lower than you estimate?) If you might be a little cooler than is comfortable for your colleagues, there are changes you can make to adjust your temperature a little higher in a way that still feels true to yourself.

Some of the suggestions I offer to those clients who want to make sure they are projecting warmth include the following:

1. Ask warm questions. Make the effort to ask genuine questions about others at work. Ask questions that help you keep up with the lives of colleagues, not only questions driven by business.
2. Practice careful listening skills. Listen to what is being said and convey support and encouragement rather than receiving information passively or criticizing. Offer suggestions, if it seems appropriate.
3. Be mindful of body language. I regularly catch myself crossing my arms across my chest in a posture that appears closed off. Simply learning to keep your arms at your sides is one way to convey openness. You can also demonstrate empathy through eye contact and

tone of voice.

4. Watch your email etiquette. In email correspondence, take a moment to say hello, ask a warm question, or offer a note of appreciation. It's not possible for every email, but make it a habit as often as you can.
5. Find opportunities to include behaviors at work that come from the heart rather than the head.
6. Focus more on being interested than interesting.

Some leaders, like Ellen, just don't think in terms of warm questions and comments. If that's you, these examples can help with both in-person and email conversations:

WARM vs. COLD QUESTIONING

COLD	WARM
Did you get the work done?	How did the work go today? What was challenging about today's work? Is there anything I can do to help?
Why was the project late?	What happened with the project timeline? Tell me about the challenges.
I don't agree with the decision or the direction this project is going.	I understand there was a lot of thought that went into the decision, and here is another perspective to consider.
We are in a meeting right now. Can you meet at another time?	Thanks for checking in about getting together. I would like to meet with you. Let's check our calendars to find a time that works.

WARM QUESTIONS AND COMMENTS ABOUT WORK
How did the meeting go last week? I thought you did great in that presentation. Tell me more about how it went. How is the project going? What do you like most about your job or project?

WARM QUESTIONS AND COMMENTS ABOUT LIFE OUTSIDE WORK
How was your weekend? How was your spring break? Tell me about your trip. What was the best part? What is your favorite place to visit? How is your family? What are your kids involved with?

For Ellen, I knew email was part of her everyday communication, so I suggested we discuss what was wrong with her current email style and how she could make it work well for her as a way to stay connected to others at her job.

"It's a great tool for people who are busy and work alone a lot," I explained. "It's also great for introverts, for whom too much in-person interaction is draining."

I've had clients whose emails were literally one word long. Those notes were reactive, and they didn't offer anything to connect us. I'm not suggesting we return to the art of Victorian-era letter writing, but if a leader's emails are repeatedly one sentence or just a word or two, they may not be sending the right signals.

Ellen knew she wanted to change the impact she made, so she thought a lot about what signals she wanted to send. She thought of those like a traffic light. She wanted to send a green signal, because she really wanted to come off as approachable. Sometimes she used another traffic light color, red, to stop herself when she was writing about sticky topics, giving herself time to think about how she could warm up her writing to better make her point. She even changed her font size, which was minuscule, to something people could actually read. She tested it out on her sister Anna to see what she thought.

"She loved it," she told me at our following meeting. "She keeps joking about this as my communication makeover, like on those television shows where someone gets pulled from a crowd and the consultants get rid of her dowdy clothes and unflattering hair." She shrugged, and I laughed.

Ellen's head-down, hard-work style really showed when she went beyond even what I suggested and reached out to everyone who had given feedback to tell them how helpful their words had been and to let them know that she had not realized how she came across. She asked them to give her honest feedback if she was coming across as too brash, abrupt, or distant—to tell her if her emails didn't land right. "I really care," she said. "I don't want to show up this way."

That vulnerability alone softened the hearts of the people at work who had judged her harshly, I learned. The CFO told me that they were becoming friends. "She didn't seem to like me before," he said, "but she has told me several times now how grateful she is for my leadership, and I've been able to fully appreciate the value her science brings to the company."

SKILLS FOR CLEAR COMMUNICATION

 SENDER

Share INTENT ("Why it is important for me to tell you this.")

Ask for IMPACT ("How does it feel to hear this?")

LISTEN

 RECEIVER

LISTEN

PARAPHRASE ("This is what I heard you say . . .")

SHARE what you heard "between the lines"

Share IMPACT ("I feel . . . to be hearing this from you.")

Often we assume that our intentions are obvious to other people. We also assume that the impact we think we are having on others is the actual impact we are having on others. Frequently, we are wrong in our assumptions. By making each of these explicit, we can reduce tension and improve the clarity and effectiveness of our communication. Practice sharing your intentions (why you are sharing this information) and the impact another person has had on you (how you feel or the sense you make of what they have said).

Where Is Ellen Now?

Ellen has become adept at using personal touches. Driven to succeed, she's harnessed that part of herself to take on the task of showing warmth like she would with any other important assignment. Human Resources is happy and her boss is happy too, because Ellen's intellect is a treasured asset.

Along with this success, Ellen also thought more about what is right for her based on a deeper understanding of who she really is. She recognized she might be happier long-term if she owned her own business or worked more in the lab, where she has less personal interaction. Knowing herself more deeply may eventually lead her away from her current job.

Reader Assignment

Do you know how you show up in the workplace? How do you think a coworker would describe you? How about a brother or sister? How do you show up similarly or differently in your family and at work? Would people describe you as similar to or different from Ellen? How do you feel at work right now? What is that feeling telling you? Is there a conversation you need to have, and, if so, with whom?

TEAMS AND TRIANGLES

JAKE GREETED ME AT THE door to his office with a warm smile and enclosed my hand in an even warmer handshake. "Come on in!" he said. "I'm looking forward to working with you after the good things I've heard about you." My newest client appeared to be in his midthirties, fairly young to already be the head of marketing for a high-fashion retailer.

"Would you like something to drink?" He opened a glossy black minifridge stocked to the brim with bottles of Italian sparkling water, fresh juices, and other healthy options. Jake had contacted me after his boss had suggested that a coach could help him create cohesion in his team. I knew from the culture of this company that the suggestion of coaching probably meant Jake was struggling.

As we sipped our drinks, Jake laid out his worries. One of the most pressing, to his mind, was a problem with a newer team member, Stephen, who had approached Jake behind the scenes several times to register complaints about Mark, another employee. Jake, my client, thought he had bent over backward to see all sides of the problem between Stephen and Mark and counsel them both, but somehow his intervention wasn't helping.

"Stephen seems to really be having a hard time," he told me. "He hasn't been here very long, and Mark is already challenging him a lot. So I had a talk with Mark. I tried to be really honest with him about the situation and the importance of helping Stephen get settled in here. But Mark just complained back about Stephen. I really want everyone to be happy, but I don't seem to know how to do it."

I suggested that I gather data by talking to others in the office to unearth the most important issues. I also explained a bit about the concept of the triangle in the work context.

Most of us have been in Jake's shoes. Maybe we have two friends and, when one complains about another, we take it upon ourselves to let the other friend know there's a problem. Or maybe our mom complains that our brother isn't calling her enough, so we call our brother to tell him to step up to the plate. Triangles are common.

For the Stephens in a triangle, talking to the boss is a way to avoid conflict while still feeling like we are accomplishing something. Stephen feels tension that needs resolution, but he is not ready to talk to Mark directly. He hopes that talking to Jake will change something without the discomfort of a direct conversation.

That's obvious motivation for being in a triangle. Jake's motivation for taking on the role of middleman is less obvious, but he, too, is making a choice to participate. Why? Sometimes being the confidant, and perhaps even protector, can be a comfortable role, even if it is one that the middleman complains about. Jake's new employee, Stephen, is looking to him for help, and that gives him a connection and a feeling of knowing Stephen better. When Jake goes a step further and talks to Mark on behalf of Stephen, he may feel a sense of power based on having knowledge and perhaps a chance to change the situation.

I'm not saying that Jake is happy about his role, but he is, at the very least, accepting it.

There are moments when accepting the role of middleman makes sense. If this is a serious workplace issue (harassment, for instance), a triangle—or even a more multisided shape, with a trip to HR—is required. But for many other conflicts, someone in Jake's shoes can choose instead to listen to Stephen with empathy and care, help him clarify the problem, and then point him back toward Mark to have a direct conversation.

If Jake proposes this and Stephen feels he lacks the skills to resolve the situation, another option would be for Jake to invite both men in for a meeting to help facilitate the conversation.

There are significant reasons for Jake to tackle this problem when it comes up, and they go beyond this one group conflict. Triangles emerge often, particularly during times of stress or change when people may feel confused or anxious, and they can have serious consequences if they become part of the culture of an organization.

CHARACTERISTICS OF A TRIANGLE CULTURE

- More time and energy spent on negativity than finding and creating solutions
- Focus is on what's not working versus what is working
- Whining and complaining are reinforced with attention
- Battle lines have been drawn, and those on opposite sides view the other as the enemy
- Colleagues bond around their unproductive patterns rather than their characters, strengths, and talents
- People do not feel valued
- Someone is singled out as the scapegoat and is held responsible for what is wrong in the work environment
- Gossiping

To understand how that happens, it's useful to learn why triangles are so appealing. In sociological terms, a one-on-one relationship between two people is a dyad. Dyadic relationships are considered to be fragile and unstable, because with two people, each is dependent on the other for ongoing cooperation. If one person stops cooperating, the relationship falls apart. Forming a triangle can add stability to relationships.

Triangles are also appealing in other ways. They can help a person feel connected by talking about the other person to a third party. Managers may form triangles to talk about direct reports, because it is hard to address problems openly in front of others. Others may initiate triangles as a way of finding a mediator. Left unaddressed, triangulation can become the dominant culture in an organization.

When this happens, it can do real harm to an organization. As people talk indirectly, information no longer flows and clarity is lost. Serious issues go underground and, if triangle culture persists, this becomes normalized.

THREE REASONS WE LOVE TRIANGLES

The human tendency to form social triangles can cause communication problems. I often find that there is low awareness of the triangles people are forming in the workplace. Why are they such a sneaky and seductive form? There are three main reasons for the triangle's workplace appeal:

1. **They are a way to feel like we're accomplishing something.** Max is working on a team with Kathy and Jen. If Max doesn't like how Kathy is acting and chooses not to talk to her about it directly, he may instead approach Jen to complain about Kathy's behavior. It could be a healthy move if Max is talking to Jen only to get clear about how to handle the problem more directly, although it would probably be wiser for Max to seek clarity outside the team. Unfortunately, most of us aren't really seeking clarity in

that situation. We are talking to a third person because we would rather not tackle the problem head on. If possible, we'd love to never have to talk to Kathy about her annoying emails or the fact that she's slacking off on the current project. Approaching this third party is a way to feel we are moving forward with this problem we know must be addressed. We may even hope that this third party—especially if it's our boss—will form the third side of the triangle and fix the problem for us.

2. **They feel powerful or comforting.** If we are the Jen in the triangle—that is, the one who is being approached for help—it may feel good to be confided in and asked for help. Max and Jen could form an alliance, bonding over a secret grievance. Or, if Jen decides to talk to Kathy on behalf of Max, she may feel a sense of power.

3. **They alleviate tension.** Direct conversations can threaten our identity. What if that person doesn't think I'm nice anymore or tells me I'm mistaken, and I have to question my beliefs about myself? Even if you're someone who can handle being direct, you may feel unprepared to manage the feelings of the other person once you tell them how *you* are feeling. All this wondering and worrying (not to mention the problem behavior itself) builds stress and tension. Forming a triangle with a third person to talk over the problem lets off steam.

———

As I talked about triangles with Jake, he looked troubled. And he was still worried about what to do next.

"I have to talk to Mark again," he told me. "Stephen told me Mark is now being dismissive of him since I had that conversation. I thought I was helping! Do you have any tips on how to handle my conversation with Mark?"

"I think you could talk to Mark," I said. "But I think what would be most helpful is if you encouraged Stephen to have a direct conversation. He can then get his needs and wants known. It will help them build a working relationship."

"I wish that would work," said Jake. "It's difficult for Stephen to do that as a new employee."

"My concern is that if you go talk to Mark, then he feels there's more talk about him behind his back. It creates more distrust within the system and more distrust with you."

"Well, I'll ask Stephen," he said. "You're right that I have to get out of this triangle somehow."

"Give it a try, and see what happens," I said.

Jake did not look relieved as some would be when given permission to put work on someone else's plate. His eyes were serious, and his voice softened. "I'll try," he said.

"How do you feel about asking Stephen to do that work?" I said.

"Honestly? Uncomfortable," he answered. "I feel like this is part of my job to take charge of issues and help my new employee make a smooth transition. It doesn't feel right leaving someone new like Stephen to fend for himself. Mark can be tough."

"That doesn't sound easy," I said. "Will you give it a try? And if it isn't working, we can discuss a different strategy at our next meeting."

"Sure," he said. We sipped our classy sodas in silence.

He looked worried, and I wanted to reassure him. "We can work on the triangle," I said. "And it will get much better. Some of the work will come from you. Are you willing to take a look at yourself in this as well?"

Jake nodded, but the grimace on his face suggested to me that he wasn't so sure about that idea.

In the coming weeks I learned through my fact-finding that several employees were frustrated with Jake, because complaints never led anywhere. "He always seems to listen to me and says he'll do something about the problem, but nothing ever changes" was a story I heard from several employees. Some said things had gotten worse as Jake tried to help Stephen and Mark get along. Trust was low, and problems were being swept under the rug.

I gradually unearthed that Jake was a very good listener and appeaser. Good listening is an excellent trait, but in triangles, what you do after you listen also matters.

At the next meeting Jake gave me another delicious beverage and an excuse I have heard from many triangle participants before.

"So, how did it go with the triangle?" I asked. It was very comfortable here, tucked into an armchair with a bubbly drink. I could see why Stephen might want to run to this office for help.

"Well, I didn't have time to deal with that yet. It's just been a mess around here," said Jake.

I nodded, and I felt some empathy. I've said that line myself when faced with an unpleasant task. "You have a big job," I said. "It's understandable that you wouldn't have a lot of time. Is there also a part of you that might have been avoiding the conversation with Stephen?"

"I guess so," Jake replied. "But I really didn't have time." He wasn't looking at me now but looking out the window at a view of the mountains. I imagined he'd rather be somewhere far away right about now. He sighed. "But do I want to have the conversation? No, I don't. In fact, I kind of changed my mind. I think I should go ahead and talk to Mark instead. I know Mark can be a challenge for some people, and I also know he'll listen to me."

My job in a situation like this is not to try to force Jake to do something he doesn't want to do. The coaching session belongs to him, and if what I'm suggesting is not working, I will try another way to keep things moving forward.

"I think you should go ahead and do what you feel is right," I said. "Try that, and we'll evaluate it later."

Jake looked relieved. We talked about the rest of his work, which was a pleasure for him. My client was so sharp and personable that he easily drew in new clients, and his elegant presentation was a perfect fit for his job. I hoped we could work out the problems with his team, because, aside from that issue, Jake seemed to be just where he belonged.

Jake Breaks the Triangle

It was a couple of weeks before I saw Jake again. He had just returned from a successful business trip in Europe and offered me some French chocolates from a beautiful gilded box. But I had a feeling he wasn't thrilled to see me, and I figured that was because I kept reminding him of the problem at work that he would rather not consider.

"Did you manage to talk to Mark?" I asked.

"I did. Things didn't go so well," he said.

"I'm sorry. Tell me more," I replied.

"When I tried to talk to him, he got defensive and said that he doesn't have a problem, nor does he know why Stephen would have a problem with him. He said he had no idea there was an issue. Then, when I told him I was surprised that he was unaware, he seemed angry."

"What did he say?" I asked.

"He said, 'Why won't anyone ever just tell me when they have a problem?' Then he reminded me that this had happened last year, which was something I'd forgotten."

"What happened then?" I asked.

"Well, Rachel—who isn't here anymore—had come to me to say that she couldn't tolerate Mark taking credit for her work. She felt it had happened more than once. When I talked to him about it, he said he hadn't realized he had been doing that. In the end we worked it out, but he was always irritated with Rachel after that. She got her credit, but they didn't do well as a team."

"What do you think is happening?" I asked.

"I only know that the team is fractured. I don't know. I am great at my job, but I can't handle all these egos very well. What do you suggest?" said Jake.

"At this point, I think the best thing would be to get you, Mark, and Stephen into a meeting together. What do you think of that?"

"If you think it will help, I'm happy to do it."

We scheduled a meeting for later that week. Stephen and Mark walked into the conference room, greeted me, then said curt hellos to one another and took seats on opposite sides of the table. Jake sat down next to me.

He introduced me to the two of them and then began to introduce the topic, which was the plan we had discussed. "Melissa is here to help me. I really want our team to be cohesive and aligned, and I want to make sure we can talk directly."

I saw Mark shoot a look at Stephen, who was, thankfully, watching Jake speak. "I've asked Melissa to speak and support us to ensure that communication is clear and everyone feels heard."

So far, so good. We were all nodding, except Mark. He looked eager to talk.

"Mark, did you have something to say?" said Jake.

"I'm glad you want us to feel heard, because I don't understand what's going on," he said. Mark wasn't particularly large physically, but his voice was booming and his face tensed in a way that looked aggressive. As he talked, he looked directly at Stephen, and Stephen appeared to shrink back into his seat. Stephen was one of the most creative people at work, Jake had told me, but he appeared to be conflict-avoidant.

Before we encouraged Stephen to talk, I wanted to get an explanation of triangles out on the table. When they are normalized and people I coach begin to understand how common and appealing they are, they can see the triangle as something other than their personal failing. It's a trap we fall into, and changing our behavior can stop the problem.

I described the triangle and how typical it was in teams. I also said that we wanted to align these two first and then move to the greater team. I let them know that they weren't exceptions, and that the issue of triangles was a common one in businesses and in the rest of life.

I got up and drew out the triangle in order to depersonalize it.

"Here is what happens in a system," I said. "A has an issue with B. There's tension between A and B, and B wants to relieve the tension, so B talks to C." I explained why we all get caught in them. As I talked, I could see that both Mark and Stephen were visibly relaxing. At one point, Mark laughed. "I think I have this with my wife and daughter," he said. Stephen smiled and nodded.

Jake and I had talked about the importance of getting Stephen to talk directly to Mark, and now Jake stepped in.

"Mark, I know what you mean," he said. "The more I've thought about this triangle thing, the more examples I can think of in my own life. And I didn't even like taking geometry." He turned to me and joked, "Thanks a lot. The other night I couldn't get to sleep, trying to remember what a scalene triangle looked like." He laughed. Tension in the room was slipping away.

Jake was in his charming element, and I was afraid for a minute that he would fix the problem without ever getting Stephen to speak up, but he followed through just as we'd discussed.

"So, Stephen," he said, "this is about the cohesion of the team. We all have triangle issues. I'd like you to talk to Mark about the issue, because, as Melissa has explained to me, continuing with the triangle isn't good for the team."

Stephen cleared his throat. "Mark, I've been trying to work with you, and I'm feeling resistance. You're not returning my emails, you're never around when I need an answer to my questions, and when I try to follow up, you seem put out."

THE SOLUTION TO TRIANGLES

We often group together in threes. Triangles are stable geometric forms (at least when they aren't resting on a point), and are such a natural part of life that few people notice when they are in one. We've all heard of "love triangles," but we also form nonromantic triangles with our families, with our friends, and at work. For example, a boss might have three employees working together on a team or two employees who are in conflict and turn to the boss for help.

Since triangles form naturally, leaders must eventually learn how to manage them to create a healthy, productive work environment.

Here's a typical triangle work scenario:

Sue thinks her coworker Lucy is being too harsh on her at team meetings.

Sue wants Lucy to change. Instead of talking to her, she decides to go to her boss, Bill, to complain.

Sue's boss has a talk with Lucy to try to solve the problem.

What's wrong with this arrangement?

Most people prefer to scuttle sideways away from conflict like a threatened crab. But allowing triangles to form usually creates new, bigger problems. X is disempowered by not having the conversation and stating his truth. For her part, Y no longer trusts X, because he has gone behind her back to complain. Intentionally or not, the two are more likely than ever to clash. Meanwhile, the boss is taking time away from other tasks to step into the triangle and setting a precedent for future conflicts.

The solution?

It depends on the problem. If this is a serious workplace issue—harassment, for instance—a triangle is required. But for many other conflicts, it is usually most healthy to listen to X, the employee with issues, and then point them back toward Y to have a direct conversation. If employees lack the skills to resolve the situation, it might help for the supervisor to bring them together to initiate the conversation.

If you are in a triangle, think hard before asking others to intervene on your behalf. Taking charge of the situation by being direct—even if it's uncomfortable in the moment—will help clear the air and will also increase your confidence.

Stephen, with help from the rest of us, had begun to dissolve the triangle that had formed. The conversation was not easy for a little while, but with the understanding that we have all been seduced into participating in a triangle at one time or another, everyone seemed to take the problem a little less personally.

When I saw Jake again two weeks later, we had rhubarb sodas, and he described how things were going. "You'd be so proud of me," he said. "I caught myself engaging in another triangle, and I did it differently this time. It was a lot easier putting a stop to it right away rather than waiting for things to fester."

HOW TRIANGLES WORK

- A & B experience "static" in relationship (frustration, conflict, annoyance, disappointment, etc.)
- A tells C about B
- C is now "triangled" in

Triangles occur when two people experiencing tension or "static" in their relationship deflect their energy to a third person (or thing) rather than dealing directly with one another.

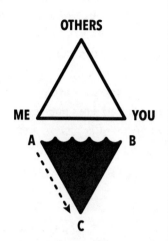

IMPACT ON INDIVIDUALS

- A and C feel closer, and C can feel important or valued
- C can feel distance or a reaction to B from indirect knowledge
- A and B experience short-term decrease in discomfort (because tension is going to C)
- A and B avoid conflict
- A and B develop long-term inefficient and unempowered (but perhaps stable) patterns of functioning
- C feels tension of (or even responsible for) A and B's relationship

IMPACT ON SYSTEM

- Lack of trust (ripple effect)
- Decreased capacity for change
- Inefficient processes
- Norms are developed to support indirect communication

Where Is Jake Now?

After a few setbacks, Jake learned how to break some of the triangles among his team members and found a way to shift some of the responsibility back onto those employees so they could reclaim their own power. He had a bigger opportunity to use his new skills the following year when he got a new job at a cutting-edge retailer, where his team was also mostly new. He began right away to structure the team so they'd have more opportunities to connect with each other. They even get together socially, as well as have team meetings without him. He tells me they are performing more highly than he had ever anticipated. He's had to get used to the compliments from others on team cohesion and to the quiet around his office. With that space, he's found himself developing the most creative marketing plans of his career.

Reader Assignment

Where are you participating in triangles in your life? Which part do you play in the triangle? What's one thing you can do to break this triangle? What could you do differently to keep new triangles from forming?

BLIND SPOTS

KIM CALLED ME IN A panic. She was a client I had worked with a few months previously, and the first time I met her, I was wowed. She seemed to have endless promise as head of sales at a manufacturing company, with an Ivy League degree, the persuasive skills of a diplomat, and an intelligence that missed nothing. However, I soon learned she had a problem following through on promises. We had worked on this issue in the first round of coaching, with satisfactory results.

It seemed that the change had not been lasting. "I'm worried that I'm going to lose my job," she said on the phone. "And I'm hoping that if I get more coaching, maybe I can stop that from happening." She told me that she knew she was letting people down again. "I don't exactly know why I'm doing that, except that perhaps I'm under too much pressure. I just know I'm disappointing people."

After setting an appointment with Kim, I hung up and considered the situation. I wondered what might have gone wrong and if there was something we didn't tackle in our previous coaching sessions. Why wasn't this working out for her? Had we failed to identify a problem? I hypothesized that during our previous coaching Kim had been able to comprehend on an intellectual level the changes she needed to make, but that she hadn't fully grasped the interior barriers getting in her way. It would take more coaching for me to see if I was correct and, if so, what those barriers might be.

I had learned from colleagues during the first round of coaching that despite her strong sales skills, her coworkers had begun to lose their trust in Kim. Several people she worked with regularly complained about tasks she had promised to take on and never completed. She was also known for missing deadlines, and when this came up in meetings, she would push back and set the blame elsewhere rather than taking responsibility. Yet after our coaching, she really seemed to take the issues to heart and had offered apologies to several people who were angry. She had begun to make changes to become more reliable with her work even before our few months of coaching ended, and she had seemed sincere in her desire to do better. I had left feeling hopeful.

Now, several months later, Kim was more upset than I'd ever seen her.

When I met her for coffee near her office, she told me more about what had happened. "I'm ashamed to say it," she said, "but I let more emails slide. And then I was late with the quarterly sales reports."

"That happens sometimes in business," I said.

"No, but I was really late," she said.

"Why do you think this happens?" I asked.

"I just get caught up in my own work," she said. "And I don't like to say no when people ask me to deliver."

She asked me if there was anything I could do to help with this. I offered her more coaching sessions and said that I did believe she could make some changes, but that it probably wouldn't be very easy. Was she up for that? She said she was.

On my drive home, I thought about the concept of the leadership brand and how that fit into her dilemma.

Your leadership brand is what people say about you when you're not in the room. Your brand is not based only on tasks or on results, but on your behavior on your way to those results. How am I interacting with others? Am I behaving in a way that is consistent with how I'd like to be seen? Brand = behaviors + results.

We already had insight into how others saw Kim when she wasn't in the room. I suspect many people had been surprised when they discovered that her supercompetent, fast-thinking, Ivy League brand could disappoint them. How did she want to be seen?

When we met a few days later in an office conference room, I discovered that Kim had had a meeting with her boss. He had told her several of the complaints and stressed that these were not minor, particularly since they were the same complaints that came after her last coaching session. Her boss warned her that things needed to improve significantly. She needed to clarify what she could do and follow through.

"How did that news feel?" I asked.

"It was awful," she said. Yet she looked more clear-eyed than she had previously appeared at the café. She was no longer distraught. "But I guess in some ways it was a relief to get this on the table," she said. She brushed her hands over the desk in front of her, like she was sweeping the problem away.

"I knew I wasn't following through with my other responsibilities," she said, "but I just tried not to think about it."

I asked her how she kept from thinking about it, and she said that she threw herself into the sales work and that it would make her forget for long stretches of time that there was anything going wrong in the rest of her job.

"Where did you learn that technique?" I asked.

"It's not a technique." She shrugged. "It's just what I do."

I knew, though, that people often learn coping techniques early to get through difficult situations. During our last coaching session Kim hadn't wanted to talk about her past, but with her job on the line, she was now willing to reach back into the past. After some discussion, she decided to open up. She spoke quietly, but her gaze was steady.

"I guess the technique must have started early on," she said. Kim had been the oldest child in a household with a single parent who was mentally ill, and from an early age she had been expected to hold the family together in ways most children are not. With a strong intellect, she was able to get perfect grades while also managing meals and housecleaning when her mother was unwell. She was frequently exhausted, she said, but she pushed through that feeling in order to succeed and to take her younger sister along with her, giving her the love her mother often couldn't. Now, years later, she was still trying to maintain the same pace and still felt that if things went wrong, it was her own fault. She was used to always saying yes to taking care of everything, but behind that she felt resentment.

"So you were a survivor," I said.

She looked nervous. "Yes, I guess," she said. "I had to survive. I had no choice."

We talked about how that felt, and then I asked her how it tied back to what was happening at work. "Is that what is happening now in your work? Are you trying to survive?"

"I guess," she said. "I mean, I'm also trying to get better results and get things done."

"Tell me more about not getting back to people," I said. "You know that's central to the feedback you've had. What happens there?"

Kim told me she didn't want to let anyone down. "I mean, I know the delay must be frustrating, but I really will get it done. That's my intention. Sometimes it's on the shelf for a while, though—it's not a priority."

I asked if she had thought about just telling someone that she couldn't get it done in their time frame and naming a date that would work for her.

She sighed. "Melissa, you don't know what it's like here," she said.

"Tell me your experience," I replied.

"If I tell them it will take a while until I do something, they'll be let down. They'll be annoyed too. It's not an option."

We talked about what might make it an option, and then she agreed to give it a try.

However, based on her brand, I suspected it might be some time before she was able to take this step. Kim's history had led her to being terrified of having open, honest conversations, feeling vulnerable, or asking for any help. She couldn't actually do everything she was promising to do for her colleagues, but to tell them so was too dangerous for her. She kept her head down and worked on what she could control as an act of self-preservation.

SAY HELLO TO YOUR INNER CRITIC

I work with many highly talented, high-performing executives with proven track records of success. Inside, however, they don't always feel secure.

The inner critic is something most of us carry around. It's that voice that nags you, saying you're not good enough, you're going to be judged, and you should probably just keep quiet right now. Sometimes it feels like my inner critic isn't just one voice but a full-sized marching band.

So I can relate to my clients who have accomplished a lot and yet hear the inner critic whenever they try something new. Sometimes the way we react to the inner critic turns out to be another way we beat ourselves up. "Why do I have to always be so negative? Why can't I be more confident all the time?" Other times we react to the critic by ignoring the voice and pushing down the feelings of self-criticism in order to get through a meeting, a conversation, or a day.

There's another approach, and when I or my client can pull it off, it seems to have the best result. Try saying hello to your inner critic. Get to know what the critic is telling you and how you feel. "There it is again, that self-doubt feeling. I always get that gnawing in the pit of my stomach and that inner voice telling me I can't do it." You could even give your inner critic a name. When we feel and name the discomfort, it seems to have less power over us. Once you've felt it, recognize that it's a common, normal part of being human.

From this compassion will come the courage to be imperfect and to go ahead, take risks, and remain open despite what the inner critic will have to say about it.

———

It was a few weeks before I found out what Kim had done next, because I had a hard time getting a meeting with her. She would ask me to propose a meeting time, say yes to it, and then cancel at the last minute. Work commitments, weddings, illnesses—the reasons piled up, and I started to feel firsthand the frustration of her coworkers.

Sometimes, if we don't follow through, the message we send is "I don't care." Is that the message we want our colleagues to hear? I knew enough about her to understand it was more complicated than that, but her colleagues did not.

I began to wonder if I would be able to see her again when one day she called, asking to set up an appointment. She named a time when I happened to be free and, within a week, we were sitting across the table from one another. She wore an elegant suit, her hair swept up tidily. I remembered that my first impression of her so many months ago had been to feel a little intimidated. She was so polished, down to the manicured hand I was shaking at that moment. But what she had to say showed that, behind it all, she was feeling vulnerable.

VULNERABILITY AND TRANSPARENCY: LETTING PEOPLE SEE WHO YOU ARE

"The difficult thing is that vulnerability is the first thing I look for in you and the last thing I'm willing to show you. In you, it's courage and daring. In me, it's weakness," writes author Brené Brown.

With their peers, some people are naturally able and willing to be vulnerable and transparent about their thoughts and motives. But for many people, this is difficult. They worry others will see their vulnerability and try to take them down. Believe it or not, vulnerability and transparency aren't signs of weakness but more like superpowers for leaders in the workplace. They are abilities that will guide a leader and a team to greatness.

Her boss had gotten very quiet for a few weeks. She had asked him about a meeting the three of us were supposed to have, and he had not replied. I told her he hadn't communicated with me either. She said she had panicked after a while and asked her boss what was going on. He had told her they weren't sure if it made sense to have a group meeting, because they hadn't seen much change in her since we'd begun working together again.

"I'm starting to really worry," she said, and I thought she might be close to tears. "I think I'm about to lose my job."

I already knew the answer, but I asked anyway. "Did you try asking one of your colleagues for more time when they requested something from you that you couldn't carry out in their time frame?"

"No, I did not," she said. "As you can tell by what my boss said about change, I messed up again. I agreed to make changes to a report, and I lost it in my inbox because the deadline was during a work trip." She sighed. "I mean, of course I should never have said I could finish a job that week," she said. "I was overloaded! I don't know why I said yes."

I was going to ask her if she would try again to set her own terms and take the fallout, but she had already figured that out and beat me to it.

"I know. I should have done what we talked about. And I will do it now. But will I lose my job before then?"

"I don't know what your boss has in mind," I said. "But making this change will be about more than today, right? This is about changing the way you do things. No matter what you do next, you'll need to make this change to move forward, right?"

She agreed with me.

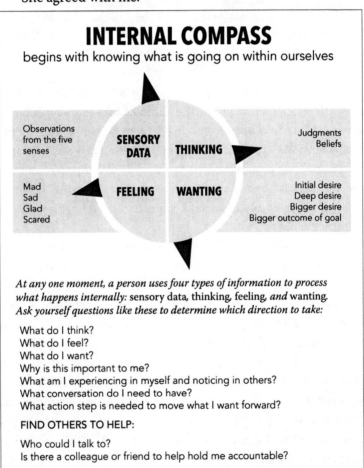

INTERNAL COMPASS
begins with knowing what is going on within ourselves

| Observations from the five senses | **SENSORY DATA** | **THINKING** | Judgments Beliefs |
| Mad Sad Glad Scared | **FEELING** | **WANTING** | Initial desire Deep desire Bigger desire Bigger outcome of goal |

At any one moment, a person uses four types of information to process what happens internally: sensory data, thinking, feeling, and wanting. Ask yourself questions like these to determine which direction to take:

What do I think?
What do I feel?
What do I want?
Why is this important to me?
What am I experiencing in myself and noticing in others?
What conversation do I need to have?
What action step is needed to move what I want forward?

FIND OTHERS TO HELP:

Who could I talk to?
Is there a colleague or friend to help hold me accountable?

I asked Kim to do one more thing: to pay attention to the requests she gets from colleagues and write down how it feels when she responds. What does it feel like to say no? What does it feel like to say yes when she knows she probably can't carry out her end of the agreement?

We didn't set a meeting that day, but within a week I heard from Kim suggesting a couple of dates for our next appointment. This was promising. We only had to rearrange them once, and that was because her boss had sent her on a trip she hadn't known about before—a totally legitimate excuse.

When we met in the conference room, Kim's shoulders were more relaxed than I remembered, and her face looked calmer than I'd ever seen. Before I had even begun to ask about her progress, she started to tell me about what happened.

"Well, I actually did tell one of the people on my team that I couldn't do something," she said.

"Wow," I said. "That's great news!" It sounds like a funny thing to celebrate, but this really was great news. It's not easy to push back.

"Yes. Alan asked me to look over some work and weigh in with substantial ideas by the end of the week, and I told him that I could do it, but that it would take me until next Wednesday rather than Friday."

"How did he take it?" I said.

"Not well." She didn't seem particularly upset about that. "He said it wasn't acceptable. And I know what you're wondering. Did I cave? No, I did not. I had to bite my tongue, though. When he first asked me to do it, I really, really wanted to say yes."

"What did that feel like, saying no?" I asked. "Did you keep track of how it felt in the moment?"

"I did," she said. "I've even looked over my notes a couple of times. I didn't so much worry that I was letting him down, I felt sad that I was letting *me* down. I want to be able to do it all, you know? I felt a little sad."

She was doing more than most people already, and I now understood her motivation. She seemed to understand it better too.

"It was terrifying, in a way," she said. "I was afraid I'd lose my job if I negotiated. And I did think about what you and I discussed at our last meeting about my childhood. I even remembered something I'd forgotten. When I was a teenager, my aunt took me to this support group for kids with mentally ill parents. I only went a few times, but I remembered that they talked about how kids in that situation often find themselves trying to make everything perfect, when perfect is impossible. They're just working hard to make things seem normal, I guess. Of course, I do that. I just haven't thought about it in a long time. I suppose I wanted to forget about that history."

I could imagine she did. And I was delighted she felt enough confidence in me that she could share her thoughts and feelings on something this sensitive.

LEARN TO RELY ON YOUR INNER COMPASS

"Follow your inner compass" sounds like simple advice, but it can be difficult in practice. We learn our gut instincts over years of trial and error, but at the same time the rules we learn to get by with others often include tamping down those instincts. The less we rely on the compass, the harder it can be to use it when we need it. The inner compass can lead you where you want to go. Here are some ways to start doing that.

1. Set aside time to think about who you are and what you want, whether for a few minutes a day, or an entire vacation. Take the time you need to answer some of those questions without interference from others.

2. If you know where your compass is pointing you but aren't going there, figure out why. Just knowing the reason, whether it's because you're scared, lazy, or angry at a lack of good options, will open the door to making a move.

3. Find someone you trust who will hold you accountable, such as a friend, partner, colleague, or coach. They can help you sort out what's important and, when you make a decision, help make sure you follow through.

4. Follow through. You could start with a small decision, but make sure you are taking some sort of risk. After you've followed your intuition, reflect on the result. Did it turn out as you wanted? Would you do it differently next time? How did it feel to take that leap?

The more you do this, the easier it will get. You'll be able to look back at past successes and thank your inner compass for being true.

I was also relieved that she had had the work conversation she needed to have. To tell someone at work that you can't fulfill a job they are asking of you is not easy for many of us, but Kim had extra trouble with this because of her history. Having done this once, however, and having paid attention to how it felt to do that, she had taken a big step. I was hopeful that this would stick.

"And you know what?" she said. "The conversation with Alan weighed on me for a couple of days. I actually almost called him back to say I could do it after all. But after that, well, I felt some freedom. Like I could concentrate better on the work I really had to do."

She told me she knew she would now be able to deliver to Alan on time—the time she had chosen. She said she was already ahead of schedule.

"I hope that my changes will help," she said.

"It seems you're setting a new dynamic here," I replied, "and that should serve you well." We spent the rest of the session discussing her leadership brand, and as I left, she spontaneously hugged me. "I'm just so happy to make this change," she told me. "I want to send the message that I do care and that I'm honest, even if that causes a little bit of discomfort."

Where Is Kim Now?

Kim still sometimes has to catch herself when she starts to say yes to something she can't possibly do, but she has told me that the more she practices saying no, the easier it is. One coworker who had been frustrated with Kim's inability to follow through on promises has now become one of her close friends. I saw them having lunch together when I was in for a meeting with a different client. "She thought I was a rival for her job," said Kim, "and that I was undermining her on purpose. That was so far from the truth!" It seemed that once Kim admitted she couldn't do everything perfectly, connections to coworkers became easier, and this new friend had recognized how much the two of them had in common.

Reader Assignment

We can get so focused on what's important to us that we forget what's important to other people. What would you want people to say about you when you're not in the room? What do you think they would say?

FINDING YOUR VOICE AS AN INTROVERT

SIMON IS WELL-RESPECTED, LIKABLE, HANDSOME, and highly introverted. Introverts can be spectacular in leadership roles, and Simon rose quickly in his career in finance for tech companies because he is a fantastic thought leader, stacking up accomplishments in his own reserved and quiet way. Simon's company had asked for my help, because they wanted him to be a top executive but weren't sure if he could summon the assertiveness to really lead.

When I met Simon, I was drawn in by his quiet authority. He spoke slowly and thoughtfully, and as we walked through the hall to his office, I had to slow down my brisk stride to meet his pace. Simon's office appeared to be his sanctuary. It was neat, well furnished, and decorated with a few large plants, which I came to think of as a green screen, sort of like the pleasant distance he kept between himself and others. There were also a couple of small, subtle landscape paintings on the walls. I commented on how much I liked them, and Simon told me that he had thought about becoming an artist before getting his degree in finance. He still painted whenever he had time.

We talked a bit about some of the ambitions the company leadership seemed to have for him, and I asked him what he thought about taking on a larger role.

He steepled his hands before him in thought, then shared his answer.

"I'm interested in it, because I love this company. I do wonder if I can do it in the way they would like."

I asked him to tell me more about this.

"I am aware that some people on my team are unhappy. I've been told I could boost confidence by having more meetings, but I really can't understand how that would help," he said. "I do my best work when I'm alone, and that's what they've hired me for—the results I bring."

"What do you think they really want?" I asked.

"Well," he said, "to be honest, I know it is part of my role leading the team. I need to connect better with people. And I try to. I really like everyone here. I just tend to keep my thoughts to myself. Please keep this in confidence, but I actually sometimes wonder if I could find a job like this where I don't have to have any meetings at all." He looked over at one of his paintings, landscapes with no people in them.

"Not a fan of meetings, are you?" I asked.

"Well, I like some meetings," he said.

"So when are they a problem?" I asked.

"This could be a long answer," he said, once again pausing to think. Then he reeled off a list of types of meetings he hated, delivered in a semi-joking tone. It did make me laugh. He didn't like meetings if they didn't require a necessary outcome or decision right now. He also didn't like impromptu meetings, because he wanted his ideas to be well thought out, and he wanted to present them carefully. He didn't like meetings where he was required to speak a lot, because he didn't like listening to himself talk—it wasn't interesting to him.

I smiled. "And the meetings that aren't a problem?"

"The short, infrequent ones," he laughed. "But like I said, I actually love this company. I think we're doing great work. I am just not sure what I can do differently and still feel like myself."

It was interesting that he wasn't seeking attention, because the spotlight found him anyway.

After our initial meeting, Simon was scheduled to present to a group down the hall, and I was invited to go along to observe how he connected with an audience.

It was fascinating. Simon expressed himself beautifully, like a brilliant professor talking about his favorite subject. His hands waved and passion glinted in his eyes as he shared his expertise. The audience was silent, anxious to hear his thoughts. Colleagues, direct reports, and his boss all eagerly listened to what he had to say.

After the presentation, several people approached him to ask follow-up questions. It was then that he seemed to switch gears. He kept gathering up his papers while he chatted, and I heard him promise several people he would email them answers to their questions later, but that he had to go. As he passed me, he shook my hand courteously and agreed to set up an appointment for two weeks later.

ARE YOU AN ASKER OR A TELLER?

Leaders tend to either "ask" more or "tell" more. Sometimes they do neither and keep their opinions to themselves. These differences in personality all have particular strengths, but lean too far in any of these directions and problems with connection can occur.

One leader leans too strongly to connect and is experienced as too mushy, with no backbone.

Another leader is always telling and taking strong positions, coming across as an arrogant know-it-all.

Very quiet leaders may seem either overly pliable or distant and arrogant.

Effective leadership is about balancing these possibilities.

People often know where they fall in this description, whether they are very connected and don't express many strong opinions, too distant and extremely opinionated, or some other combination of these traits. Some need to work more on the soft skills of listening, empathy, and storytelling, while others may need to push themselves to take a position and share an opinion and idea.

Once you know yourself, you can more quickly sense what to do next in any particular moment. If you're an opinionated "teller," you can assume that the next time you're struggling to connect with someone, leading from the heart or asking a good question is likely the most prudent path. If you're someone who connects well but you find yourself nodding and asking questions all through a conversation or meeting, it might be time to float some opinions.

The ultimate goal of this work is to make effective connections, stay curious, state thoughts and feelings, and honor all perspectives.

During the interim, I had interviews with some of the people he worked closely with: direct reports, his boss, and others who came in contact with him. I heard it was typical for Simon to go straight back to his office after a meeting. More than one person told me they weren't sure if he liked them or just tolerated them. "He's hard to read," one woman told me. He often canceled meetings with direct reports or moved meeting times around. At the same time, Simon was actually well-liked. I suspected he had become successful this quickly without generating resentment because he wasn't trying to grab the spotlight. What I heard in interviews told me that others wanted to feel connected to him and, through him, to the business. I wondered if Simon would be willing to make that leap.

It was clear to me that Simon was an introvert. There's a misconception that introverts are shy people. That doesn't capture what makes introverts different from extroverts. Introverts may not be shy at all, but they tend to prefer environments that are quieter and lower-stimulation. Much of their best work is done alone. These personalities can be misunderstood, particularly in the modern American workplace where communication and assertiveness are often valued as highly or more highly than creativity. Add in an open office workspace where an introvert can't ever be alone, and most businesses are likely not getting all they could from their introverted employees.

Simon seemed fairly self-aware already, and he knew that quiet and solitude were critical to his work. He had his own office, which is fortunate, and he was also important enough to be able to turn down meetings when he wanted to. But knowing that I'd been asked here to help him with leadership skills, I felt sure it would be hard for him to rise any further in the company if he didn't communicate better with his employees.

Simon stayed focused in areas where he felt the most comfortable. At our meeting he had told me that he was always asking himself, "What can I get done to move the business forward?" Unfortunately for the bigger picture, all his ideas were things he—or someone else—could do alone.

I could help by teaching him some practical ways to engage more with others as long as he was interested in making that shift.

SHOWING UP AS INTROVERTS OR EXTROVERTS

As writer Susan Cain has argued persuasively in her recent book *Quiet: The Power of Introverts in a World That Can't Stop Talking*, introverts, who prefer environments that are quieter and lower-stimulation, are often underappreciated in the modern workplace, because standing out and communicating are valued more highly in big business than contemplation and solitude are. Even office design, which is currently trending more toward open, collaborative workspaces, can work against the quiet that would support more introverted employees.

In an extroverted culture like the average American workplace, there is likely to be a need to give some thought to the needs of introverts. If you are the boss, you can do this by providing some quieter spaces, but also structure meetings to make sure introverts are invited to share ideas. You might offer multiple opportunities for sharing creative ideas and opinions rather than expecting introverts will deliver their ideas during one fast-paced meeting.

If you are an introvert, you may need to practice skills—speaking up, for instance—that are not inherently comfortable but that may be necessary in your workplace. Introverts, who may not easily find opportunities to connect with others, can use scheduling to correct the imbalance by planning ahead to meet with peers and direct reports. They can also find unique ways of making connection. One example Cain gives is of an introverted leader who loves his employees and writes handwritten notes to express his appreciation.

At our next meeting, I told Simon some of what I'd discovered. He was surprised to learn that people really wanted to spend more time hearing from him. He thought he was telling them enough. He knew meetings were something he needed to do more of, but he hadn't recognized that the motivation behind many of these gatherings was the desire for other employees to have time to talk with him and learn from him.

"This might sound silly, but I've never really understood why people want more contact with coworkers," he told me. "They already have all the reports and other information I've given them. Wouldn't they rather just get out of here and be with their families and friends?"

"Believe it or not, Simon," I said, "they actually admire you and want to hear what you have to say."

Simon had been trying to lead from his own belief system. There was a pretty large gap between what Simon needed and what others needed from him. He was a rare case—a person who didn't need attention, connection, and validation from many others. Some people really do connect closely with only a very few important people and are content that way.

"So, more meetings?" he asked.

"Well, yes and no," I answered. "You will need to get together with people more than you do, but also, you need to find ways to share what you're thinking. Do you do that already?"

Simon thought that sharing his reports and having strategic meetings with his boss and a few other higher-ups fulfilled his duties in that regard. But I pointed out that his peers and direct reports seemed like they would actually be inspired to work harder if he kept them abreast of his thinking.

CONVERSATION
In the present moment

PAST ----- **NOW** ----- **FUTURE**

Conversations here are about:
What happened before (often based on recollection)

Conversations here are about:
What is happening NOW, between you, me, and the team:
"I" statements **(WHO)**
Specific information **(WHAT)**
Right here **(WHERE)**
Right now **(WHEN)**

Conversations here are about:
What will happen in the future (often general and abstract)

Conversations in the present are more intense. Though it's easier to talk about the past and the future, talking about what's happening in the here and now helps individuals and teams move forward. To spend more time in the present, ask yourself questions like, "What am I thinking?"; "What am I observing?"; "What emotion am I experiencing right now?"; "What exactly are we discussing and what does it mean to me? to others?"; and "Have I shared 10 percent, 50 percent, 80 percent of what I think about this issue?"

The following week Simon had another meeting, but this time he did it a little differently. First, he set aside time at the end of the meeting for questions. Second, he began to reach out to his direct reports for coffee appointments. At those appointments, he could have one-on-one meetings that allowed him to make connections with these important members of his team, and he could do it outside the office and in a controlled amount of time—always important for him.

The coffee idea was based on another discovery we had made, which was that in some situations Simon was more extroverted, relaxed, and assertive, and those situations were almost always outside the office. Therefore, any way he could find to participate in off-site meetings, coffees, or even informal after-work gatherings offered great opportunities for him to connect with coworkers.

Simon was able to do this because being a good leader was important to him. In the book *Quiet: The Power of Introverts in a World That Can't Stop Talking*, author Susan Cain describes a highly introverted professor who is able to regularly give public speeches, because he had chosen to act like an extrovert for the sake of something important to him, a phenomenon called Free Trait Theory. Writes Cain, "According to Free Trait Theory, we are born and culturally endowed with certain personality traits—introversion, for example—but we can and do act out of character in the service of 'core personal projects.'"

Simon could do this in service to his job, which meant a lot to him. It was also important to him to let others in the company know that they were valued. But there was one more strategy we needed to use in order to make Simon feel fully comfortable.

In the same vignette, Cain describes how the professor builds lots of quiet time into days when he has to speak in public or meet with a group. He even goes so far as to hide out in a bathroom stall just to have alone time! I thought we could find a better escape than that, and we did. There was an art gallery across the street which often featured artists Simon admired, and Simon decided to make it a ritual to go out for a coffee about an hour before his larger meetings. He would then duck into the gallery to gaze at—and occasionally purchase—the art on the walls. Those moments lost in art seemed to recharge him. After the first couple of trips, the gallery owner (perhaps an introvert herself) had sensed his desire to be alone with the paintings and no longer tried to engage him in prolonged conversation. "Going there has saved me more than once," he told me.

Where Is Simon Now?

Simon has improved communication with people on all levels, and it appears that's given the company a lift. Retention numbers are up, and so is morale. There is perfect attendance for Simon's brief coffee talks each month with direct reports, and his quarterly meetings, where he shares his strategic thinking, leave people inspired. Now, when Simon makes a decision, he tells me he is mindful to communicate it to his team, and he thinks it is helping them feel included. Simon has discovered that even his peers are looking for that inclusion, so he seeks opportunities to have lunch with them. He admits that this is in the service of what others want. "I'm happy holed up in my office," he says. He likes his work, though, so he's willing to make these compromises to succeed at his company. He has also found even more ways to carve out time where he can be alone. He told me that he can get drained by the increase in lunches and coffee meetings, but that after a couple of months of doing this, he approached his boss and got permission to work from home at least twice a month. Simon says almost all of his most innovative ideas have emerged during those hours at home.

Reader Assignment

Do you think you show up as the same person at work as you do outside of work? Who is the person at work? What do you love most about this person? What situations make you feel at your best, and at what times does it not quite feel like you? What do you love most about your outside-of-work self? What do you like least? If you were to integrate the best of both selves, what would that be? How would you show up more fully? What keeps you from doing that now? If you were to address it, what could you change or work on?

BUILDING A CULTURE OF TRUST

MONICA, THE VICE PRESIDENT OF global marketing at a food industry firm in Los Angeles, was warm and engaging, with an infectious laugh and a fondness for telling a good story. Monica's creative energy and drive had helped her to achieve enormous success in her field, sometimes outshining more-established leaders. Still, tension had been developing with some of her direct reports, and her company's Human Resources office strongly suggested that Monica receive coaching. They wanted her to understand the issues of her direct reports and the rest of her team.

After I took on the job as her new coach, I met with Monica and several of her colleagues. That's when I was able to see the flip side of Monica's exciting, overflowing temperament. My client liked to have a lot of control. Her assistant explained that when the florist bought in a fresh arrangement each week, Monica always stopped by the front desk in order to move the vase. To the left. To the right. She liked things to be just so.

Monica's direct reports told me that she also liked to have a say in everything her team was doing. This was a particularly difficult problem, because Monica's primary job responsibility was to generate and develop creative ideas and connect with the company's top clients. She had risen in her career because of this ability, and it was her creative work that inspired her most. That work kept her busy enough that she often missed looking over the work of her team before their deadlines were looming or gone. One of her direct reports, Helen, was a rising leader in the company. She told me Monica was as fun and exciting as she appeared, but that over time she had begun to wish for a more boring leader.

"She rarely shows up at meetings, but she wants to look at everything I'm doing and sign off on it, and she takes a long time to get back to me. She almost always has suggestions for a change—usually late on Friday afternoon. It's stressful. We're always waiting to hear whether she'll say yes or no." She told me she had the feeling that Monica didn't trust her to follow through on her work. "I think I've been reliable," she said, "but it almost feels like she expects me to fail."

"I do think she cares," said Flynn, one of her employees. He then told me about the third time that month Monica had made last-minute changes that would stall his most important project for another month.

"She seemed genuinely apologetic. I just wish she could let go and let us take more control of our work. We really are good at what we do," he said. "She recruited me, after all! I just need some trust."

Now, at my meeting with Monica, we were going to talk about some of this feedback. I hoped to encourage her to delegate some of her decision-making to others.

With a warm smile, Monica greeted me in the lobby of her office building, and I followed as she walked briskly to her office. The wall behind her desk was decorated with vibrant photos she'd taken on the scuba-diving trips and epic mountain climbs that she took on her vacations.

As I settled in, she took charge of the conversation. "I've heard there are frustrations," she said. "So let's get right to it. What can I do to fix this problem?"

"What are the problems you have identified?" I asked.

"You know, I haven't found anything I consider a real problem," she said. "But I'm open to the coaching process—it seems like it could be valuable. I know my direct reports would like to see some changes, so I was hoping you could tell me what I can do that would be helpful."

I had been planning on sharing some of my findings from my meetings with her colleagues, but if she wanted to get straight to solutions, we could start there.

"Sure," I said. "From what I've learned, having more meetings with your direct reports and the rest of the team is one of the best things you can do to solve some of these issues."

She raised her eyebrows. "It seems like we have enough of those already," she said.

"Okay," I said. "Tell me about how you make time with your direct reports."

"Well," said Monica, "I have an hour set aside every week for each of them."

"Do you usually keep those meetings?"

"Pretty often."

"Would you give me a sense of how often? Is it 80 percent of the time? Maybe 50 percent?"

She looked up at the ceiling, as if thinking back over recent weeks.

"Well, I wasn't here last week for the meeting," she said. "Things come up." She raised her hands, palms out, as if to say "don't blame me." But I knew the direct reports did blame her, because without her close contact, they couldn't do their jobs properly.

"So maybe I make 50 percent of the meetings," she said. "But if I don't make it, I always reschedule."

"Do you also have team meetings?" I asked.

"Sure we do."

"Do you attend them?"

"No, the team generally meets without me."

"When they meet, are they able to get a lot done without you there?" I asked.

"I think so," said Monica. "But, of course, I do like to have final say. I think that's probably normal for someone in my position, isn't it?"

"It's hard to generalize," I replied. "But it seems like this is a bit of a bind. If you want to be the one to authorize everything, you will probably need to make time in your schedule to be at more meetings. Do you think it would help to give one of your direct reports more authority over decision-making?"

"I did think about delegating to Helen," she said. "She's doing great work. However, I'm not sure how effective she'll be without my direct oversight. I've had bad experiences before with teams falling apart."

"Would you be willing to do some delegating to Helen and see how it goes?" I asked.

She agreed that she could.

"I think she'll appreciate that opportunity, and I think you could consider setting up a meeting with her about that soon," I said. "I know you're busy right now, but from what I can see, more meetings now could lead to fewer meetings in the future."

She nodded.

Why was it so hard for Monica to delegate? I think that part of what made it difficult was Monica was the kind of leader I call a "doer." She had built her career by stacking up accomplishments, and I suspected this was what she valued most in herself at work. It was a part of her identity that extended even to her vacations, where she felt best in action. For this kind of leader, delegating work to others would feel like she wasn't doing her job. Monica hadn't yet discovered that an effective leader is not only a doer, but also one who helps others to accomplish and achieve. If a leader has a well-chosen team, they should be able to safely step back and delegate more. A great leader will learn to measure their strength by how happy people are and what kinds of results they are getting. If Monica could create a culture where her direct reports felt safe enough to be who they were and were trusted to make decisions, at least in their areas of expertise, Monica could gain pride and a sense of power in being the kind of leader who helps others shine.

At the same time, Monica might find herself better able to generate creative ideas. This was the other side of Monica's work trouble at the moment, I gathered. She was still focused on connecting with the company's top clients, but she wasn't generating as many creative ideas as she had been before, she told me. "I think I'm a bit stuck, maybe because I'm distracted by managing the team," she had said.

From what I'd heard, I suspected that Monica was *over-functioning*—that is, taking excessive responsibility for the lives of others.

When we are most successfully managing our lives and relationships with others, we are keeping our commitments and managing our time and our various central roles (parenting, work, self-care) without either chronically expecting others to manage our lives for us (under-functioning) or regularly taking over responsibilities that really belong to someone else (over-functioning). I like psychologist Will Meek's description on his website, willmeekphd.com, of a person who is over-functioning. A UF is an under-functioning person, and an OF is an over-functioning person.

"Classic characteristics of over-functioning include being overly focused on another person's problems or life situation, offering frequent advice or help to the other person, actually doing things that are part of the other person's life responsibilities (and believing that 'if I don't do it, then it won't happen'), feeling anger when help is not 'appreciated' or the UF doesn't change (or even want to), the OF believing he/she knows a better way for a UF to be living, and frequently feeling over-whelmed, stressed, and neglecting self-care."

Monica's team members seemed capable, so I didn't think she was overly focused on their work because they were not taking responsibility. Instead, it was possible that Monica was over-functioning as a distraction from the difficult creative work she needed to do.

LEADERS NEED TO SEE AND BE SEEN

There is a deep human longing to be seen. It is one of the greatest possible gifts to show others that you see them. In the workplace, feeling seen, noticed, and acknowledged for who you are by those you admire is a tremendous motivator.

To really see others we need to be interested, curious, and inquiring. We need to take note. We can do so by tracking others' concerns and achievements, expressing empathy, and letting others know that we have understood what is important to them.

Monica asked me what else she could do, besides meeting with Helen, that might reset the direction things were going, and I responded by suggesting that she could set up three other types of meetings:

- One-on-one meetings with her other direct reports
- Director meetings
- Team meetings

"What would be the agenda for these?" she asked.

"Well, part of the work here would be to get some of your team members to set the agenda themselves," I explained.

"Oh, no," she said. "I tried that before, but we got off track."

"What happened?" I asked.

"Well, I didn't feel the agendas were capturing all that we needed to do, so I went back to setting the agenda myself," she said. "But I took input from everyone! I told them all to email me with their suggestions."

Monica said no one really understood all the things she did at work. As we talked it through, though, we found a couple jobs that she might accept passing along to others. We agreed on a couple things she would delegate before our next meeting. Then we talked about when she would set times for some of the other meetings I'd mentioned.

"I'm pretty booked up for the next couple of weeks," she said, "but I can set up a team meeting for the end of the month. What do you think? Is that a good start?"

"Based on what I've heard, I think you need meetings on the calendar for this week and next. I'd advise making room for these over some of your other appointments."

Monica pushed back, saying she really didn't have time. There was absolutely nothing she could drop off the calendar, but she would prioritize this when her to-do list was empty.

"Of course, it's up to you," I said. I was worried that she wasn't taking this seriously enough. "However, as your coach, with what I've seen, I do think you could try to get at least two meetings on the calendar between now and our next appointment." We were meeting late the following week.

Monica agreed to this and said she had to end our meeting a few minutes early. She said she was looking forward to seeing me again and was sorry she had to run.

FEELINGS IN THE WORKPLACE

Recently I was listening to one of my clients as he explained to me that his boss had not supported him in a recent meeting. He said it was becoming a pattern.

"How does that feel?" I asked my client.

"Oh, you know, he acts like this all the time. It was expected," he said.

My client was missing valuable information here about his own experience.

"Did you feel relieved or disappointed?" I asked.

"I guess I felt disappointed," he said.

From there, we talked about what that disappointment meant—the client wished his boss supported him more—and we talked about other feelings he might have about the situation. Together we helped him to reach some clarity, and he began to think about what he could do to change his work life for the better.

There's a misconception that we are not allowed to feel in the workplace. But every thought is connected with a feeling, and often our actions—in the workplace and the rest of our lives—are based on these feelings. Even if our feelings aren't named, they are present. When we don't identify them, they can become barriers to progress in the workplace.

One of the most powerful things I can do with teams and individuals is to help them identify feelings, particularly feelings that are happening in the present moment. Whether those feelings are "I'm excited," "I'm frustrated," "I'm feeling sad today," or some other emotion, they provide information that can be used to make changes.

Do you know where you fall in your ability to access your feelings? Do you know how you are currently expressing feelings in the workplace? Are you aware of the difference between a feeling statement and a judgment, thought, or opinion statement? Clarity of feeling is an enormous strength in life, well worth the work it takes to get there.

When I saw Monica again, I was curious to hear how the meetings had gone. Monica said she hadn't had time for them, and one reason was that she had lost a key colleague.

"Helen has quit the team," she said. "And she told me it was because of my lack of leadership. I'm in shock."

It was startling news, but I imagined Helen had been thinking about this for a while.

"I'm sorry," I said. "What are you feeling about this?"

"I don't know," she said. "I have too much to do to think about that. Helen has left more on my plate than I can handle."

"How does that feel?" I asked.

As with all leaders I work with, I knew that getting into the feelings of the moment was a good way to gain self-knowledge, which could eventually lead to connecting better with others.

Monica stopped restlessly tapping her fingers and spoke a little more slowly. "I'm overwhelmed. I felt I was doing the best I could. I guess I'm shocked."

"It must be hard," I said. "What do you think was really going on with her?"

She shifted around in her seat. "I don't really understand this line of questioning. I have more to do than I can handle right now just thinking about how to replace her."

"Well," I said, "I think it's really important to this process to think about what was going on with her to prevent this from happening again. If you had to put yourself in her shoes, what do you think she really wanted and needed from you?"

Monica was always moving, acting, and expressing, and my goal was to slow her down enough that she could connect with what had been happening at work.

Monica didn't like to talk about her own feelings, but I suspected that she hadn't only been surprised by Helen's decision to leave, she had also felt hurt.

"I think she was pretty clear about how she felt," said Monica. "She didn't think I was leading well."

"Was she clear about what was missing?" I asked.

"She didn't say much. She complained to me before about my not being available enough for decision-making, but I think that's unrealistic." Monica said that even though she was very busy, she did try to be as available as possible for her team. She seemed like she was trying to convince me that it couldn't have been her fault. "I have even stayed late before to talk to Helen," she said. "In fact, after she last told me she wanted more attention, I actually had her over for dinner to discuss how things were going."

I could see that Monica was not quite ready to give up on being in the right.

"That is all true," I said. "But as your coach, I do think it would be valuable for you to try to figure out what Helen was thinking and feeling. What do you think she needed that she wasn't getting? What do you think it was like for her to leave?"

Monica stayed with our conversation, though our meeting was running long. She probably really did care, just as Flynn had told me.

"I know it was hard for her to leave," said Monica. "One of the other team members is actually one of Helen's best friends. I thought she got along well here."

"So, what do you think she needed?" I prompted again.

She sighed. "Maybe a little more commitment from me," she said. "I did just remember one really difficult moment. Helen asked me to come to a team meeting when she was going to present her ideas for a marketing strategy for one of our newer clients." Monica shook her head. "I forgot to go. It seemed like she avoided me for a while after that," she said. "I did feel bad. I think I just take on too much sometimes. Overcommitment is a weak point of mine. I have a lot I like to accomplish."

"That sounds like it could have upset her," I said. "Did she ever say anything about it?"

"No, but she did email me later. She didn't mention that I'd missed the meeting, but she asked me if I could give her my feedback quickly, because she didn't want to be late with the client. She was very short in the email. I think I may have underestimated the impact it had on her when I didn't show up."

"It is possible," I said. "What do you want to do about it now?"

"I have already failed to do it," she said, tapping her pen on her desk. "If I had had those meetings, I could have talked to Helen." She sighed.

"Would it feel worthwhile to you to have meetings with others?" I asked.

"Well, I don't want to lose anyone else," she said. She shrugged. "If it will help, I'll do it."

I was happy she was going to take action, but I also knew some self-reflection would help her to make the more lasting changes that were needed. I thought it would be helpful if we understood why it was hard for her to delegate, so I asked a few more questions.

"What do you feel when you think about handing off more work to someone else?" I asked.

"Well, it feels a little odd, if you must know," she said. "I know delegating is supposed to be a part of leadership, but I'm in charge. I shouldn't be handing off my jobs to others. I like to be accomplishing things, anyway. That's how I got to where I am."

I nodded. "You have done a lot," I said. "And I'm told you have a lot to do, generating creative ideas and meeting with the big clients. Is it hard to do that at the same time you manage everything else?"

Monica looked at me, clear-eyed. "You know, I think it's impossible."

"I know that accomplishing more is a measurement some leaders use for success, but at your level, sometimes leaders start to also measure their success by the kinds of results their teams deliver. How would it feel for you to try to aim for that goal rather than doing it all yourself?" I asked.

In previous meetings I'd become accustomed to Monica's distracted style as she was jotting notes, rushing out to talk to someone who walked by her office, or getting interrupted by a phone call. Now, though, she was as still as I'd seen her. "With Helen leaving, I can't do it all anyway," she said. She pointed at the list she'd made of meetings to set up and told me she was ready to move forward with a bit of delegation.

NEW RESEARCH ABOUT WHAT MAKES A GREAT LISTENER

Research shows employees value respect from their leaders above all else, yet over half of employees don't feel they get that respect.

I have learned that full, engaged listening is one way leaders can show respect for others, and nothing breaks it down for me more clearly than the Japanese kanji symbol for listening. The left side of the kanji represents the ear. The right side is you—your attention, your focus, your eyes. In the middle is the heart. If

EARS

EYES

UNDIVIDED
ATTENTION

HEART

you are listening with your ears, your eyes, and your heart, your employee is more likely to feel that they have your undivided attention and your respect.

There is also new research about what makes up good listening. Two writers, Jack Zenger and Joseph Folkman, analyzed data from a development program designed to help managers become better coaches, identifying the leaders who were considered the best listeners and sifting through their listening behaviors to identify the difference between great and average listeners.

Some of us may have been coached in the rules of good listening, which typically comes down to staying quiet and not interrupting and sometimes repeating back to the other person what we have heard them say. ("It sounds like you wish I'd wash the dishes more often. Is that right?") But in Zenger and Folkman's research, they found that the leaders who were considered the most effective of all were involved in more of a two-way conversation. As they describe it, "The highest and best form of listening comes in playing the same role for the other person that a trampoline plays for a child. It gives energy, acceleration, height, and amplification."

Some of the behaviors of effective listeners include the following:

- Asking good questions that showed they'd been listening
- Conveying support and encouragement rather than passive reception or criticism
- Making suggestions

The last behavior was surprising to the researchers—and to me, actually—because a common complaint about bad listeners is that they try to jump in and solve the problem rather than listening. The authors analyzed the data this way:

Perhaps what the data is telling us is that making suggestions is not itself the problem; it may be the skill with which those

suggestions are made. Another possibility is that we're more likely to accept suggestions from people we already think are good listeners. (Someone who is silent for the whole conversation and then jumps in with a suggestion may not be seen as credible. Someone who seems combative or critical and then tries to give advice may not be seen as trustworthy.) "What Great Listeners Actually Do," by Jack Zenger and Joseph Folkman, *Harvard Business Review*, July 14, 2016

For a longer discussion of this subject, see Matthew Kohut and John Neffinger's book, *Compelling People: The Hidden Qualities That Make Us Influential* (2013).

When we met the following week, Monica told me she had set up the meetings I had suggested, and she wanted more coaching on the subject. "In fact, I'm talking to Flynn this morning about taking on an expanded role," she said. "I hired him because he's great at his job, and I don't want to lose him too."

She also said that she'd finally had time to prepare for a meeting with the executive team and board. "I spent a couple of days reflecting on where we need to go, and I even began to research some of the ideas I've been scribbling down in a notebook for the last few months," she said. She had a vacation coming up—a yoga and surf retreat in Mexico—and she planned to get up each morning and generate some creative work. She would give Flynn a bit more responsibility and see what he could do.

Where Is Monica Now?

Monica is learning to slow down and pay attention to her impact. She tells me that one of the first questions she asks herself in the morning is "What can I delegate?" "There's a saying about accessories," she told me. "Put on what looks right to you, then remove one thing. That's what I'm doing with my to-do list—well, maybe two things off." She told me she's finding pride in being a good leader and in being needed in a different way than before. She is also finding new wellsprings of creativity. By listening more fully, being present with her team, and cultivating the talents of her employees, she's building a culture of trust.

Reader Assignment

Do you over-function in your life? If so, in which areas? How does over-functioning help you? How does it hurt you? How does it help or hurt others?

Or do you under-function? If you developed your career as a doer, is that still appropriate to your current role? Or have you moved up to a management role where you need to develop skills in delegating and encouraging leadership from others?

CULTIVATING EXECUTIVE PRESENCE

"I JUST DON'T FEEL JOY in this job anymore."

I was sitting in a windowless conference room with my new client, Derek. It felt a little stifling, like the heat was on too high, and Derek, a big man, seemed equally confined by the office chair he'd chosen to sit in. There were two nice armchairs across the room, and I suggested we move. He agreed politely but without much enthusiasm. He had soft features and a gentle manner, and I immediately felt we'd get along.

When we sat again, I waited for him to continue. I'd been told this software engineer for a major retailer had a lot of talent and that his team really loved him. Yet he was not happy at all.

"I just want to get better results," he said. "But I can't seem to motivate my team."

This was similar to what he'd told me over the phone recently when we'd discussed his motivation for seeking coaching, and I was ready to hear more. There can be a lot of reasons a team is not motivated. I needed to learn more about Derek to see what we should focus on.

"I'd like to learn more about you," I began. "For example, what do you think of as your strengths?"

He smiled. "Well, I think my strength is that I'm really good at software engineering. It's exactly what I was meant to do. I loved it in school, and I love it now!"

"That sounds pretty joyful," I said. "What about your strengths as a leader outside your technical work? What do you think those are?"

Derek cupped his hands around his cheeks and sighed. "One of my strengths is also one of my problems, I think," he said. "Everyone says the same exact thing about me. I'm 'really nice.'" He rolled his eyes. "I have to say, I don't feel very nice at the moment. My team is barely keeping up with the schedule for the project we're supposed to be completing, and I've been putting in extra time."

I was starting to get a picture with these comments. Being liked is important for an executive, but it's not news that people who are liked a lot sometimes struggle with being respected. It depends on whether or not the likeable person is willing to take a stand. I suspected we might want to look for opportunities for him to do so in a way that was authentic to his real self.

"What are you feeling, if not nice?" I asked.

"I'm feeling frustrated," he said. That made sense, given his situation.

"Anything else?" I asked.

"I want to be respected enough that my team will be motivated, but I do want to be liked, I guess."

As I thought about Derek's dilemma—being liked but not respected—I was also giving some thought to the topic of executive presence. "Executive presence" is a phrase used in coaching and in organizations to refer to a quality that is expected of top leaders.

I knew Derek's frustrations had a lot to do with wanting to be one of those top leaders. He hadn't gotten that invitation yet, and he was looking for reasons why. Derek was able to do his technical work exceptionally well, but he sensed there was something missing in his leadership, and I could tell he suspected it had to do with this nice-guy image.

Being a nice guy is not actually a drawback, despite the image that phrase conjures up. The jerks in the business world do sometimes get ahead, but in the end I don't believe they are truly respected, and egomania does not tend to command real loyalty over the long term. On the other hand, a nice man or woman can command a very deep loyalty and respect, but only if the niceness is coupled with some sort of strength or force. The kindness needs a structure to hold it up—like an airy chocolate soufflé that rises in the strong dish that holds it, or a silk blazer that requires crisp shoulders to counterbalance the fluidity. It's the yin and yang of personality.

Executive presence is like that too. It seemed to me that our coaching would need to address Derek's executive presence in order to help him move upward in the company.

We made an appointment for two weeks out, and in the meantime, I had evaluations with his direct reports. They hesitated to say anything negative about him, which made it difficult for me to learn much until I met his direct report, Wendy. Wendy told me that she was ambitious and that she would let me know what was wrong, because she also wanted to move up in the company, and she felt that the weakness in their team was not giving her a chance to show off her gifts.

"Basically, Derek and I do most of the work on the team," she told me. We sat in the same two chairs in the windowless meeting room where I'd sat with Derek, but Wendy's presence was completely different from Derek's. She was energized, sitting near the edge of the seat, meeting my gaze with a confident look of her own. She spoke in a lively voice and aired her opinions with strength.

"I'm tired of us doing all the work on the team, but I report to Derek, and I don't think it looks good for me to jump in and push the other team members. That's his job." Still, she had nudged other members of her team a couple of times, because Derek wasn't making his authority felt, she said. "Please don't share this, but I'm thinking about transferring to another team," she said. "One where the leader does a better job of holding everyone accountable for holding up their end of things."

BOLSTERING YOUR EXECUTIVE PRESENCE

In coaching, I regularly see very talented leaders whose ideas are critical to a business but who, nevertheless, have not yet been invited to the executive team. It's hard to imagine anything more frustrating at work than making huge contributions only to be held back. What can be particularly difficult in these situations is that often higher-ups explain the leader's failure to move forward with one of the vaguest explanations in the business: He/she lacks executive presence.

Sorting out the meaning of this catch-all phrase can be quite difficult. That's because "executive presence" as a term seems to vary according to who is being told they are lacking it. Usually, though, it's not impossible to figure out. My clients and I can often sift through feedback, ask more questions, and discern the areas we can work on to strengthen executive presence.

Here are a few reasons leaders I've met have been seen as having a less-than-executive presence:

- Coming across as "too soft"
- Seeming rigid
- Being emotionally sloppy and leaving resentment in his or her wake
- Having a sloppy physical presence: awkward handshakes, unprofessional attire, unfriendly demeanor

There are many more possible issues that may fall under the umbrella of "presence," but John Beeson, in the *Harvard Business*

Review article "Deconstructing Executive Presence," asserts that the term "ultimately boils down to your ability to project mature self-confidence, a sense that you can take control of difficult, unpredictable situations, make tough decisions in a timely way, and hold your own with other talented and strong-willed members of the executive team."

Beeson also says that executive presence will be developed "if you have a baseline of self-confidence and a willingness to deal with the unpredictable situations that go with the territory at the executive level."

I agree with this assessment, and it is why I work with clients on the issue. Your work on this issue may involve taking steps to make your voice heard and make sure your wins get attention. For others of you, it may be about learning to handle anger and disappointment in a way that shows maturity and self-possession. Changing how you act may be done in small and large ways; what is important is that those changes are authentic to your true self. If you have a gentle demeanor, taking steps to be more assertive will likely take a different form than it would for someone who is naturally tough. If you have a more, well, *sloppy* physical presence, it doesn't mean you should have an overhaul that makes you look dapper but uncomfortable.

In the end, I believe executive presence is about projecting yourself as a confident, respectful leader in a way that is authentic to who you are.

We met at a coffee shop for our next appointment. Derek might have felt okay in the windowless office, but it didn't feel right to me. I asked Derek what it was about being called "nice" that bothered him.

He thought about it. "I actually want to be liked," he said. "But I feel like it's the only thing people have to say about me. I'm a lot more than that, but it's as if the niceness makes it so they can't really see me."

"When do you experience that?" I asked.

Derek had a perfect example for me. He said that last quarter he had won an award from a software engineering organization for some of his work, and his boss had pulled together a group to celebrate after work. Over cake and glasses of wine, his boss had raised a toast. He'd said a small amount about Derek's talents, and then he'd said the thing that drove Derek crazy, "It couldn't have happened to a nicer guy." Nothing about Derek's hard work or any other aspect of who he was. Where were the details on exactly how he'd won the award? The details about his wins?

Derek and I went over the anonymous feedback I'd compiled and, as it confirmed, he was thought of as a nice guy. But he was surprised to hear that not everyone saw that as a positive attribute. I told him I had heard that his niceness might be making life more difficult for the harder-working people on the team, because he wasn't holding other team members accountable.

"Does that ring true to you?" I said.

Derek thought about it and seemed a little hurt. "Everyone should want to do more. Should I really have to prod people to do things right? I guess I grew up thinking that you did the right thing and worked as hard as you could for yourself. How can I make other people work hard if they don't want to?" He told me that his boss sometimes got loud and "shouty," but there was no way he could do that—it just wasn't who he was.

I decided it was the right time to talk about executive presence, which includes the ability to take a stand while staying connected with others at the same time, and I explained to him that building that presence was usually necessary in order to reach the top level of any organization. I also explained that for his presence, I thought it would be critical for him to take steps to make his voice heard and to make sure his wins got attention.

"What if we could find a way that you could hold your team accountable without shouting?" I asked. "Would you be willing to do that work, even if at first it makes you uncomfortable?"

"If I don't have to shout, I will try it," he said. I could hear him over the sound of the café's espresso machine, and that would have to be good enough.

ACCOUNTABILITY IN THE WORKPLACE

The goal in any business culture is to have accountability at several levels—peer, direct report, colleague, and managerial. One form of accountability is when each individual is doing what they say they will do, acknowledging when they cannot or did not follow through, and holding others to the same standards. Leaders also hold direct reports accountable. They must follow through, and if they don't, the leader must be committed to having a conversation about it. The other kind of accountability in business is personal— the willingness to own the impact of one's actions.

Unfortunately, a lack of accountability is common in workplaces. People do a lot of hoping. "I hope things will get better," "I hope he will follow through," "I hope no one will notice that I didn't follow through." At other times people deny what has happened— that they have let something slide, that they are at fault (or that someone else is), or that failing to follow through with a commitment really does matter.

The main reason leaders have a hard time holding their peers accountable for action or inaction is because having those conversations is hard. On the other hand, leaders often fail to hold themselves accountable because they might not feel full ownership or approval of a task. "I don't really connect with this, so I'll just push it aside and do the work that draws me in."

Owning the impact of our actions is often more subtle. This involves being aware of the wake you leave with your emotions, your presence, and the things you say and do or don't do. Without self-awareness, it is tough to manage effectively.

For both types of accountability, it is important to develop a threshold for having direct and honest conversations. Individuals can cultivate this skill, but it's also important for executives to develop a culture that promotes this. Organizations without a culture of open conversation are less efficient, as there is more conflict (and conflict avoidance) on the way to getting things done.

To improve accountability, begin with yourself. How accountable are you? Think about how accountable you are for your work. Then think about your social impact within the business. Own the moments when you fall short. Are you ignoring your commitments because you feel they don't matter? Are you leaving peers or direct reports confused or unhappy because of your actions or the things you say?

Sometimes leaders don't recognize these different ways of being accountable, or they do not want to own and see the ways in which they have a social and emotional impact. A lot of managers also do not like holding peers or direct reports accountable, because it is unnerving to have those conversations. It feels too intimate. But leaders are particularly responsible for doing this work, because that is how they create an open, honest culture where team members feel safe acknowledging their own mistakes and are best able to move forward.

The prominent ladder of accountability tool raises readers' awareness about human nature when it comes to accountability in organizations and how they can empower themselves to make the best choices.

At our next meeting, Derek told me that Wendy had spoken up in the meeting. "She is angry at Sean," he said. "And Sean isn't really meeting our goals for software development."

"Have you talked to him about it?"

"No, he was out sick last week."

LADDER OF ACCOUNTABILITY

Implement Solutions	**INTERDEPENDENCE**
Find & Create Solutions	• Working with others • More choices
Own It & Take a Position	**ACCOUNTABLE BEHAVIOR:** Things happen because of you
Acknowledge Reality	
	INDEPENDENCE
Wait & Hope	
I Can't . . . Excuses	**DEPENDENCE**
Blame Others	• Retreating from stress • More long-term anxiety
Unaware & Deny Situation	**ABDICATING / VICTIM BEHAVIOR:** Things happen to you

When dealing with an issue, figure out your place on the ladder, then evaluate, choose, and act in order to increase your accountability. More people on the top rungs of the ladder means increased chances of success for an organization.

"Did he warn you that he would be late in meeting the goals?" I asked.

"He did not." Derek sighed. "He's a pain. I need to do something about him." But, he said, Wendy was actually starting to be sloppy with her work the last couple of weeks. "It's not like her," he said. "She's usually the hardest worker on the team."

"Why do you think she's acting differently now?" I asked. I suspected, of course, that Wendy was getting fed up with the situation and going on a kind of strike. If her other team members weren't going to deliver exceptional work like she did, maybe she'd follow suit. Or perhaps she was close to getting another job and had one foot out the door.

Derek told me he suspected the same thing. "I wouldn't be surprised if she wanted another job," he said, "but that would be a disaster for me." Then he asked me if I thought working on his executive presence could actually help avoid that possibility.

I told him I couldn't promise that but that I did think it might help, and there was the potential to keep Wendy on board if he could get other team members working at her level.

"Then I'll do it," he said. "Where do we start?"

I told Derek I thought there were two steps he needed to take. One was in the direction of sharing his own wins with his boss.

"I heard you say that you are only known as Mr. Nice, but that you have strengths and achievements that aren't getting noticed," I said. "To get that notice, you will need to advocate for yourself."

Derek nodded.

I asked what he thought about setting up an alignment meeting with his boss to share his point of view and talk over the development plan for his department.

"That sounds fine," he said.

"As I understand it," I said, "one of your points of view is that your group's wins are not getting enough attention. Could you ask your boss to champion your department more in meetings?"

Derek said it sounded kind of pushy.

"What do you think will happen if your boss thinks you're being pushy?" I asked.

"Maybe he won't like me?" he said. Then he saw my face. I was smiling a little—in a kind way—because this was just what I had imagined he would say.

"That was a trap, wasn't it?" he said. He smiled a little.

"I didn't mean to trap you," I said. "What were you just thinking?"

"I was thinking that I'm trying not to be liked so much—or, at least, not to be liked for being nice. So maybe it's okay to be thought of as pushy for once?"

"That makes perfect sense to me," I said. "The other work you can do is to show up more authentically with your team."

"More authentically?" answered Derek. "I hadn't really thought of that as the problem. I mean, I'm authentically nice, right?"

"Well," I said, "you are nice. But as you told me yourself, that is only one part of who you are. When you are in a meeting and someone on your team doesn't deliver what they have promised, do you feel like being nice?"

"No, I guess I don't," said Derek. "I want them to be accountable. I'm just not sure how I can force them, especially given my personality."

"Could you start by getting your inner thoughts—within reason—out to your team?" I asked. "I noticed at the beginning of our coaching that you were able to pretty quickly hit upon some of what you were feeling. That's a strength, and not everyone can do that without coaching," I said.

Derek looked pleased.

"But how you are feeling isn't entirely nice. You're a little mad, right? So if you keep all that inside and only allow your nice side to show, you aren't really sharing your authentic self, are you?"

"You know, I guess I'm not," said Derek. "But will that really motivate them?"

"We can work on methods for holding them accountable," I said. "It makes sense to set up feedback timelines, milestones, and other measurements to get your team back on track. Certainly you can tell your team that there will be no extensions for deliverables, and come up with some sort of penalty. But outside of that, I think, on a larger scale, getting the response you want from your boss and from your team will have more to do with choosing to show up as your fuller self from here on out."

THE MANTRA OF BOLD ACTION

Leaders usually have confidence in some areas of their work life, but almost everyone has times when they feel less confident. Some people feel completely capable of their technical ability but struggle with speaking up in a peer setting. Others love public speaking but struggle with their one-on-one conversations and giving feedback. Some are confident in building relationships, and others are more confident in dictating strategy.

For most people, it takes urgency to lead them to take a leap. I believe it helps to orient yourself toward bold action rather than waiting for a situation that requires it. When we stay in inaction, that is our narrative. Taking action, even if it's imperfect, will change your story and build your confidence. What would I do if I were bolder? If I could let go of some of my fears, how would I show up differently? See if you can turn the volume down on your inner critic long enough to take a bold step. It could be having an important conversation or taking the first steps to launch a creative idea. A habit of action can help you create a new narrative for your career, for your business, for your life.

Once you've stepped forward:
- Celebrate every win
- Steady yourself if you get knocked down
- Remind yourself of what you believe and what you want to accomplish
- Let bold action be a mantra

Two weeks later, Derek and I met in another conference room. This one had a window. Derek said he'd sat here with his boss the week before and talked about getting more attention for his department. I asked for specifics.

"One thing I did was ask him to contact Wendy and let her know how valued she is in her position. She recently nailed a huge redesign for us, and I thought she needed to hear about it directly from him."

"Did he agree to do it?" I asked.

"Yes. She actually got an email from him today. She looked really happy," he said.

"You look pretty happy too," I observed.

He said he had been feeling a little lighter this week. "Maybe because Sean finally turned something in that was as good as what he used to do when he first joined the team," he said.

I asked for more detail.

"I thought about what we discussed, and I tried to share a little more of my thoughts at our last meeting. Then I had a one-on-one conference with Sean and let him know some of my criticisms about the work he'd done on the previous project. We established a timeline."

"How did he react?" I asked.

"He looked annoyed," said Derek.

"What did you do then?" I asked.

"Well, I felt kind of bad," he said, "but then I remembered what we'd discussed. I'm nice, but I'm a lot of other things too, and I'm ready for others to know that. That kind of helped me stay strong," he said.

If Derek could keep advocating for himself and sharing more aspects of his full self, I suspected he would be known for a strong executive presence before the year was out.

Where Is Derek Now?

It had been six months since our coaching session when a note from Derek popped up in my emails. In it, he thanked me for the work we had done together, and he also let me know that the organization had met its profit goal, even with the high bar they had set at the start of the year. "I feel like the partnerships

I created with the rest of the organization really paid off," he said. "And, since I know you're wondering, yes, I'm feeling some joy!"

I was feeling it too.

Reader Assignment

Think about how the need to be liked plays a role in how you manage conversations and relationships, including work relationships and your relationship with your boss, and ask yourself some questions:

- When, in particular, does being liked feel most important or relevant?
- In which context or contexts do you tend to hold back inner thoughts? Do you do it most with family, friends, work, team, boss, direct reports, or peers? None? All?
- If you were to share more of your inner thoughts, in which contexts does it feel more risky? What benefits could you imagine from doing this?
- How would you show up differently if you had no attachment to being liked?

If you don't feel that being liked plays a role in how you manage conversations and relationships, consider paying attention to how to manage executive presence in a way that is confident and assertive, while also being connected and showing others that you care.

CHAPTER 8

CONVERSATION CAN CHANGE THE WORLD

LEADERSHIP ISN'T JUST AN ATTITUDE or a natural ability, it requires intentionality. Each character in this book began their story with at least one issue to resolve. A common thread for these characters is that they often showed up in a way they didn't intend. *Intentions are invisible*, as I stated earlier in this book. Each leader needed to understand how they were showing up—a process of looking inward and also extending outward.

How do you want to show up? What is your inner truth? What conversations do you need to have in order to show up with intention?

Perhaps you relate to Alex. He wanted to show up as a strong, empathetic leader. Yet he was very unhappy when I met him, uninspired at a job he should have loved and stressed by his boss, John. Alex had been taking the path of least resistance: grabbing what power he could by avoiding work and becoming passive-aggressive with John.

Our most important work was to help him find clarity about the barriers that were getting in his way, and to then help him set the boundaries he needed to show up authentically. He needed to speak to his boss and overcome the fear that that conversation wouldn't matter.

Ellen loved facts, which was the lens through which she viewed the world and what mattered most to her at the end of the day. She did not understand her own impact on others and was unaware that her colleagues felt she didn't care. Ellen cared about the people around her, but she didn't think expressing empathy and caring were important parts of her job.

Ellen needed new tools in order to have clearer conversations that offered positive feedback and expressed empathy. When she learned about and used those tools, she created warm connections with the people around her, which was a goal she hadn't even realized she held before we began to work together.

Jake needed tools of another sort. This leader wanted to feel connected to others, but the way he went about it—by taking charge of every conflict—was undermining his larger goal of creating a sturdy, cohesive team. His team members felt open and close with him but not with each other. Jake needed to practice holding himself and his people accountable. This meant giving up the power that came along with being the one everyone comes to for help. With a clear understanding of team dynamics—particularly triangles—Jake was able to create a more powerful team, leading to positive results for the business.

Kim was a perfectionist who struggled to allow her vulnerabilities to be seen. Kim hoped she'd get it all done and meet everyone's needs. She overpromised and underdelivered. She tried to maintain safety by presenting to the world what she thought was a perfect image, but there was a gap between how she wanted to appear and how she actually showed up. Tapping into her inner critic and understanding the lessons she had learned in her past allowed her to accept that she was as vulnerable as anyone else.

She learned to manage conversations so that she would no longer promise more than she could reasonably give, and she became more accountable to others.

I hope introverts will recognize themselves in Simon, a leader with charisma who, nevertheless, didn't realize how much his peers wanted to connect with him. Simon wanted to show up as a leader who made others feel connected and safe, but this wasn't the way he naturally operated. One of Simon's inner truths was a need for quiet, but as a leader of an organization, he also needed to share himself with others. As he learned more about how others saw him, he also came to understand some of the gifts and challenges of being an introvert on the job. He was working toward a balance by making it a priority to more personally connect with people at work, and also by intentionally creating boundaries and setting aside regular time for the quiet introspection he required.

Monica was a leader who hadn't yet adjusted to her new level at work. Her self-worth in her previous role had been built around getting things done, and now she was trying to fit that identity in a job where it wasn't serving her. Monica's is a tale of metamorphosis, as she needed to learn how to let go of her past role and embrace a new one. Of course, like all these characters, she needed to do it in a way that was authentic to her personality. Like Ellen, she could transform by recognizing her impact and learning to show up in an empathetic way for her team. When she made these changes, she also reconnected with her own creativity.

The final character, Derek, was a big man whose presence somehow felt small. His talents were underrecognized, which caused him all kinds of frustration. The solution for this "nice guy" was not to do the opposite and become the office jerk, but to risk speaking up for himself and his team. He was able to move into a bigger role by sharing his inner thoughts outwardly in a way that was, at first, a bit forced but eventually became a habit. As he shared who he was, Derek's presence became bigger and people saw him for who he really was: a nice guy with strong opinions and ideas.

As I look over the characters, I am reminded that though each individual worked with their own specific inner truths, each landed on several key traits that great leadership requires.

Great leadership requires immense *vulnerability*. The etymology of the word "vulnerable" lies in a Latin word, *vulnus*, which means "to wound." To be vulnerable is to allow yourself to be open to the possibility that you'll be touched by the slings and arrows of life and might not come out of every day without some scrapes and scratches—mostly of the emotional or intellectual kind, I hope. Just as in love, athletic feats, and great works of art, real success as a leader does not come without taking risks.

At work, this risk is taken when you decide to get to know yourself and to let that self-knowledge guide your decision-making, no matter how uncomfortable it feels at first—following the inner compass even when it's not convenient.

Another key trait of a leader is *empathy*. Great leaders learn to imagine what it is like to be in someone else's shoes. With empathy, a leader can truly connect with the people around them and understand their own impact.

Strong leadership requires *accountability*. You're doing what you've promised and you're following your inner compass, even when it sometimes makes for an uncomfortable conversation. You're expecting others to follow through on their commitments, even if it seems easier to let things slide.

And finally, great leadership requires *conversation*. As you learn who you are and how you feel in the moment, you must talk to the people around you. Whether your conversation is more like the one Alex had with his boss, letting him know he felt unhappy and required a change, or like Kim's, acknowledging her limitations, or like Derek's, as he brought his inner

truths out into the open, you will find that taking conversa-
tional risks can lead to great rewards.

I've had the good fortune to watch individuals improve not
only their leadership abilities and careers, but their feelings
about getting out of bed in the morning. When people find
a way to show up with their full selves, they feel inspired and
motivated, engaged and alive. I hope every reader finds a way
to show up more fully themselves today and every day.

TOOLS FOR SHOWING UP

I. *Feedback Survey*

LEADERSHIP COACHING IS ONE OF the rare places where we can get honest information about how we come across to others. Leaders learn what their colleagues appreciate about their work, and also where they are not being perceived quite as they imagine. All of us have blind spots when it comes to our public identities. Others can see things about us that we cannot see ourselves. This work offers a person an opportunity to match who they feel they are inside with how others perceive them on the outside. For example, if you feel warm toward your colleagues but others find you cool, you can learn how to come across with more warmth or share your vulnerability a bit more.

It's hard to mine for this kind of data on your own, because many people are less likely to be as frank to you personally as they are with a coach and a cloak of anonymity. Still, if you and your siblings, friends, acquaintances, and colleagues can handle the impact, this feedback survey can give you very useful information. Sending your questions by email—with a promise not to get angry at the answers—might make it more likely that you'll get the truth. Just be sure you really *can* accept answers that don't reflect you as you thought you showed up. Remember, just because some answers don't match who you feel you are inside doesn't mean you aren't who you thought you were. It means you have some work to do to align your actions with your inner self.

The Questions

1. What are three adjectives that describe me?

2. What do you see are my top strengths?

3. How else could I be more effective as a father, sibling, daughter, friend, or colleague?

4. What do you appreciate most about me? Where have I been most valuable to you in our family, friendship, or work relationship in the last few years?

5. If the person filling out the questionnaire is someone you have known for a long time, also ask, What was most valuable in the relationship with me ten years ago, and how about now? What has changed or is different?

6. What can I do more of? Less of?

7. In groups, do you see me as a person who asks questions or a person who tells people about things? What's your perception of how I show up in groups?

8. Do you find me direct or indirect? Would it be helpful if I were more direct or more indirect? Do you see me as an introvert or an extrovert, or a bit of both?

9. Would you describe me as easy to know or hard to know?

10. Would you say I lead more with strength or warmth, or both?

Send these questions to friends, relatives, or colleagues you feel might answer honestly. Ask yourself these same questions before you read their answers. When you get their replies, identify the gaps between how you perceive yourself and how others perceive you. If you have asked multiple people, consider the common theme that emerges from their answers.

———

II. Keys to Managing Anxiety

One of the distinct attributes of anxiety is that it is nearly always set in the future. Can we handle what's next?

There is a good kind of anxiety that excites and prepares us for something meaningful and challenging. Then there is the unpleasant anxiety that can twist our stomachs in knots, leaving us fearful about the future. It is that kind of anxiety that keeps us awake at night and that most of us want to learn how to manage.

The first step is usually to take some deep breaths, which helps our bodies to relax.

Then we can ask ourselves if the anxiety is rooted in a serious problem that really does require help and a shift in direction or if it is something we might be able to manage on our own. Maybe I'm always anxious about work because it isn't a good situation for me. Or maybe I'm not prepared for that presentation, and I need to own up to that fact and reschedule it.

Or maybe some really difficult things are going on in my life, and I need to recognize my limits and reach out for help.

If, on the other hand, the anxiety does feel manageable, it can help to learn the root of it. Is it a fear of failure? A wish to be liked? Or a sense that you are not good enough? If we can learn about our anxiety, we may be able to honor the discomfort while still moving forward.

And this is the critical step: staying neutral, or complacent, can reinforce the anxiety. As we stay still, in our minds we amplify the risk and minimize our own capacity to be resourceful. Taking action teaches us that we can move past our anxious thoughts and feel better.

——

III. *Conversations That Matter*

Begin with Yourself: A Six-Step Process to Getting Clarity

STEP 1: Identify an issue or situation that needs to be resolved.

   a. The issue that is most pressing for me right now is:

....
....
....
....

STEP 2: Clarify the issue with the internal compass.

   a. What are my thoughts, judgments, and beliefs about this issue?

....
....
....
....

b. What do I feel?

_____
_____
_____
_____

c. What do I sense and observe with my five senses in others or within myself?

_____
_____
_____
_____

d. What do I want?

_____
_____
_____
_____

STEP 3: Define the facts.

a. What is going on? How long has it been going on? How bad are things?

_____
_____
_____
_____

b. What was said?

_____
_____
_____
_____

c. What was done?

_____
_____
_____
_____

d. *Any data?*

e. *What was not done?*

STEP 4: What are your intentions, goals, or outcomes regarding this issue?

a. *What are my intentions?*

b. *What are my goals?*

c. *What impact is this having on me and others?*

d. *When all is said and done, how will I feel and how will others feel when this issue is resolved?*

STEP 5: Reflect on your personal contribution to the issue or situation.

a. *How am I contributing to this issue?*

STEP 6: Commit to action: What action steps can you take?

a. *What are potential steps I could take to help resolve the issue?*

b. *What conversation(s) do I need to have? With whom? And what are the goals of those conversations?*

c. *When will I take these steps?*

———

IV. Starting the Difficult Conversation

STEP 1: Describe the problem as the difference between the two stories (your story and theirs).

a. Start from this third story:

....

....

....

....

STEP 2: What are you hoping to accomplish by having this discussion?

a. Share your purpose for having this discussion:

....

....

....

....

STEP 3: Ask: What are you thinking, feeling, wanting?

a. Invite them to join you to sort out the situation together. (Shift to a learning stance: listening, empathizing, paraphrasing.)

....

....

....

....

―――

V. The Role of Gratitude in Leadership

Don't underestimate the role of gratitude in improving physical and mental health and in strengthening leadership.
Psychologists have been studying the benefits of gratitude,
and this subject is also a topic of interest in the workplace as
a way to motivate employees and build first-rate teams. While
you can't fix all your problems with positive thinking, research
indicates that putting effort into feeling thankful and, when
appropriate, expressing gratitude to others can be beneficial
for health and relationships.

- Thankfulness can help you and your colleagues cope
  with difficulty. There is scientific evidence that people
  who feel gratitude can enhance well-being in a way
  that allows them to better weather stressful times, like
  when you get a challenging work review or endure a
  difficult conversation with your boss.
- Being thankful is associated with a healthier heart and
  other health benefits. For instance, a 2015 study on the
  role of gratitude in heart-failure patients examined the
  associations between gratitude, spiritual well-being,
  sleep, mood, fatigue, cardiac-specific self-efficacy,
  and inflammation in 186 men and women with Stage
  B asymptomatic heart failure. "We found that more
  gratitude in these patients was associated with better mood, better sleep, less fatigue, and lower levels
  of inflammatory biomarkers," wrote one of the lead
  authors of the paper, Paul J. Mills, PhD, professor of
  family medicine and public health at the University of
  California, San Diego. The study was published in the
  journal *Spirituality in Clinical Practice.*

- Gratitude increases your employability. I have learned through my work that top employers continue to look for strong Emotional Intelligence (EQ) in their new hires. A strong sense of appreciation is one hallmark of emotional intelligence.
- Praise and thankfulness are motivating. Giving thanks to others for their efforts is considered a "prosocial" behavior that encourages others to act generously.

———

VI. How to Make Changes That Stick

Much of this book is about making changes, and sustaining change over the long haul is difficult. Experts say you can give yourself the best chance of continuing toward your goals in a few specific ways:

1. Identify a goal, make it specific, don't make it too big, and write it down. Studies suggest individuals with clear written goals are significantly more likely to succeed than those without them. So, instead of "I'll lead with more warmth" as a goal, you might decide "I will take a moment to say hello, ask a warm question, or offer a note of appreciation in at least half of my email correspondence."

2. Learn how to develop a habit. Charles Duhigg's book *The Power of Habit* offers a scientific explanation for how our habits are formed and a model for how to create new habits. Duhigg writes, "All habits—no matter how large or small—have three components, according to neurological studies. There's a cue—a

trigger for a particular behavior; a routine, which is the behavior itself; and a reward, which is how your brain decides whether to remember a habit for the future."

3. Be patient while making a change. According to several studies, it tends to take around two months of practicing a new behavior before that behavior becomes habitual. This suggests that we should put our greatest effort at changing our behavior in the early weeks. Work hard to maintain your New Year's resolutions until the beginning of March, and they will have the greatest chance of becoming changes that stick.

4. Find activities you enjoy. University of Chicago behavioral science researchers Kaitlin Woolley and Ayelet Fishbach researched goal-setting, tracking participants who had set goals—such as advancement in career or improved health—and following up after two months to learn how successful those people were at staying the course. They asked questions such as how much enjoyment the individuals had while pursuing their goals—did they have any fun in the spin class; did they find any pleasure paying off their debt—and then further asked if they were still working on their goals. "We found that enjoyment predicted people's goal persistence two months after setting the goal far more than how important they rated their goal to be," wrote the authors in an April 26, 2017, article in the *Harvard Business Review*.

Meanwhile, they found that caring about the delayed benefits—for instance, weight loss or being debt-free—did not predict how much time or effort participants actually gave in pursuit of a long-term goal. Thinking the goal was important did not predict success. "Having fun did," the authors write.

The authors suggest three ways to use this information in pursuit of your own goals:

1. Consider what you'll find fun on the way to reaching your goals, and orient your activities in that direction.
2. Find ways to give yourself immediate benefits. (For example, the authors write, they found that high school students worked longer on a math assignment with an accompaniment of music, snacks, and colored pens.)
3. Focus on those immediate benefits, paying attention to any enjoyment in the moment.

ABOUT THE AUTHOR

Photo © 2013 Ingrid Pape-Sheldon Photography

FOR MORE THAN TWENTY YEARS, Melissa Williams-Gurian has worked as an executive coach and leadership development consultant. Her philosophy is simple: possessing a clear understanding of who you are as a person, which beliefs and values drive your actions, and how you connect with others gives you access to your full potential as a leader. Her clients include Fortune 1000 companies, CEOs, and high-level executives and their teams from a wide range of fields, including technology, manufacturing, retail, public education, nonprofit, financial services, and health care. She specializes in helping leaders build better relationships, communicate effectively, take decisive action, and recognize and change systemic issues in the workplace. She is also a professional certified executive coach with the International Coach Federation and a licensed mental health counselor who has worked with individuals, couples, and families in private practice.

Williams-Gurian holds a BS from Cornell University and an MA in applied behavioral science from Bastyr University. She lives in Seattle with her husband and three children.

CPSIA information can be obtained
at www.ICGtesting.com
Printed in the USA
LVOW12*0920300118
564517LV00001B/4/P